Parrotlets

Parrotlet Owners Manual

Parrotlet book for care, environment, training, health, feeding and costs.

by

Harry Holdstone

Table of Contents

Chapter 1: Introduction

Parrots have been popular pets for centuries, but one species has become a firm favourite with many bird enthusiasts over the last few years: the Parrotlet.

This type of parrot, belonging to the genus *Forpus*, is the smallest of all parrots. It looks like a miniature Amazon parrot thanks to its tiny stature and brightly coloured plumage. Most of these little birds have green plumage and colour mutations are rare in the wild. However, captive bred *Forpus* are found in a dazzling array of blues, peach, yellow, dark green, and white.

In the wild these active, smart, and gregarious birds live in small flocks. The only time they don't flock is when they pair off to mate. Parrotlets, like many other bird species, are dimorphic. In other words, it is easy to tell males from females using their appearance only.

This book will introduce you to these charming, beautiful birds by discussing their appearance, biology, behaviour, the food and environment they require, their personalities, and what makes them good – and less ideal – pets.

In other words, these pages contain everything you need to know so that you can decide whether this is the pet for you and, if it is, how to select your Parrotlet, what you need to buy before you bring it home, and how to take proper care of it.

All the necessary equipment, food and the general environment that has a crucial bearing on the health and happiness of Parrotlets will also be discussed.

The Parrotlet is a hardy creature. However, they can become ill and anyone who is serious about having an exotic pet needs to know what to look for and how to deal with common ailments.

I hope that you find this book both useful and fun to read!

Chapter 2: Parrotlet basics

1) Overview

The Parrotlet, also commonly known as the Pocket Parrot because of its mini size, is part of the greater parrot family. All parrots share certain characteristics: very colourful plumage, hooked beaks, and four toes on each foot.

It is estimated that there are more than 350 different species of parrot worldwide. These eye-catching birds can be large (such as the cockatoos – also popular pets – and macaws) or small such as the well-known and popular budgie and the Parrotlet, which is the smallest of all.

These little birds are native to Central and South America, Mexico, and the Caribbean Islands where they live in large groups. While many associate parrots with forests or at least highly treed habitats, their range is in fact far more diverse than one would expect.

Some *Forpus* species are indigenous to semi-arid tropical zones in Western Mexico while others are found in Trinidad, California, and extensively throughout South America. These charming birds have also been introduced into the West Indies and the Antilles.

While there are numerous Parrotlet species living in these various regions, only a very limited number have entered the pet trade: the Pacific, Mexican, Yellow-faced, and Spectacled Parrotlet.

Thanks to their big personalities, intelligence, ability to bond with their owner if correctly socialised, and attractiveness it's hardly surprising that these species are increasingly in demand.

Their size and the fact that they are far quieter than larger parrots also make them a good choice for pet owners living in apartments.

2) Parrotlets in the wild

Forpus need trees or large shrubs to nest, forage, and feed in. In the wild these very active and gregarious birds live in small flocks.

Extremely large flocks can be seen when multiple smaller flocks –
sometimes consisting of several different Parrotlet species –
congregate at the same place to drink water or to eat or remove clay
from cliffs.

They feed on fruit and seed pods in the wild. It is thought that the
reason they sometimes ingest very small quantities of clay is that it
contains minerals that these birds need. Additionally, it is possible
that the clay may be effective in ridding them of certain parasites.

Breeding pairs separate from the flock. The female leaves first to
find a suitable nesting site such as a hole in a tree which she then
prepares by cleaning and enlarging the space. Once the nest is ready
the eggs are laid and while the female incubates the eggs her mate
stands guard to protect her and the eggs. After hatching, the babies
are fed by both parents until they leave the nest.

3) Life span or expectancy

In the wild the Parrotlet has a life expectancy of up to 10 years. If
they are well cared for in captivity they can reach their 20's or even
– in very rare cases – their 30's. However, the standard range for pet
birds is 12 to 18 years.

This surprising longevity should be kept in mind when considering
these birds as pets as it means they are a long-term investment of
time, effort, and money.

4) Parrotlet appearance and biology

These birds share all the key physical characteristics with larger
parrots. Namely, they have:

- ✓ Very brightly coloured plumage
- ✓ Hooked or sharply curved beaks
- ✓ Large heads in proportion to their bodies
- ✓ Four toes on each foot (two pointing forwards and two
  backwards).

In addition, Parrotlets have short tails, black eyes, and beige beaks. As with most bird species they are what is known as sexually dimorphic. This simply means that males and females can be easily identified by the colour of their plumage. Greens are the base colours found in wild Parrotlets.

With the popularity of these little birds as pets there is a growing palette of colour mutations. Common ones include whites, blues, and some yellow colouring (known as lutino).

The brighter yellow is called American Yellow while the European Yellow is more of a pastel shade. Fallow refers to a range of beige or even greys.

Other more exotic varieties are becoming available, but they are hard to come by and, inevitably, much more expensive.

Size and weight:

Adult Parrotlets only reach about 11 ½ to 12 ¾ centimetres or 4 ½ to 5 inches in length. They weigh in at 20 to 30 grams or 0.7 to 1 ounce!

Colours and sexing:

It should be noted that full adult plumage doesn't appear until five to six months.

> ➤ *Wild / natural*: Non-mutated individuals both in the wild and in captivity are, as previously mentioned, primarily green. Males have small patches of brilliant blue behind their eyes and on their backs. The blue markings on females are paler.

> ➤ *Blue*: These birds have a grey-blue wash on their wings and backs and sky-blue face masks. In males the blue eye markings are a gorgeous cobalt. The blue in the females is paler.

> ➤ *Albino*: As with other albino creatures, these Parrotlets are completely white and their eyes are red. Males can be identified by a breeder by examining the plumage under black light.

> *Lutino*: As with albinos, this mutation has red eyes. The plumage is bright yellow. Males have white on their rumps, wings and their neck nape. Both males and females have white eye markings, but females lack the white on their wings and rumps.

Green variations:

> *Green pied*: These are predominantly green birds with a scattering of yellow feathers. The number of yellow feathers determines whether the individual is described as "heavily pied" or simply "pied".
> *Green fallow*: This striking mutation produces birds with yellow face masks, grey and cobalt necks, beige wash mantles and wings, and red eyes. Males have vivid blue eye streaks.
> *Green marbled:* This mutation used to be referred to as "green pastel". These individuals are predominantly light green or yellow and have a marbled effect on the plumage on the neck, back, and the wings. Males have blue sex markings.

Blue variations:

> *Blue fallow*: These birds also have red eyes. The face masks are very light blue, the cheeks are white, and the necks are grey or blue wash. The mantles and wings are blue with a beige wash. Males have vivid cobalt eye streaks.
> *Blue pied*: These are predominantly blue birds with a scattering of white feathers. The number of white feathers determines whether the individual is described as "heavily pied" or not. Males have blue sex markings.
> *Blue marbled:* Formally known as "blue pastel", these birds are mainly sky blue with a very light blue marbled effect on the plumage on the neck, back, and the wings. Again, males have blue sex markings.

Other mutations:

> *American yellow*: As the name suggests, these Parrotlets are entirely yellow. The mask is a dark yellow, but the colouring is far paler on the mantle, wings, and back. Males have pale blue sex markings and the hens or females have white markings.
> *American white:* These subtle birds are white with a very pale blue wash over their bodies. Unlike the previous mutations they have dark eyes. The males have blue sex markings and the hens have none.
> *Turquoise:* This is one of the most recent mutations and as a result, they are still very hard to obtain. At time of writing, breeders are working on this colour in the UK, US, and Europe.
> *Grey:* There is a grey-green mutation and a grey-blue one. In both cases the grey is more dominant than the secondary colour.

Breeders are currently experimenting with various dominant and recessive genes to produce a staggering range of colour variations. Double and even treble colour mutations are becoming increasingly common.

The current programs are creating Green Cinnamon, Green Faded, Dark Green Fallow, Marbled Dark Green, Dark Green Pied, Olive Pied, Blue Cinnamon, Blue Faded, Mauve Pied, Marbled Mauve, Cobalt Fallow, Cobalt Pied, Marbled Cobalt, American Blue Fallow, American Yellow Fallow, and Grey Pied.

A word of caution, however. Not all breeding, especially involving recessive genes, has been successful. In some cases, the resultant offspring have been weak, unhealthy birds.

5) Types of Parrotlets

There are three genera of Parrotlets. The most commonly known genus is *Forpus. Touit* is far less known and there are only two species within the *Nannopsittaca* genus. However, for the purposes of this guide only the species most commonly kept as pets will be discussed.

Forpus Coelestis / **Pacific / Celestial Parrotlet**

This species is more usually known as the Celestial or Pacific Parrotlet. These hardy little birds hail from Peru and Ecuador and live in dry regions where there are bushes rather than trees.

Reaching sexual maturity at 10 to 12 months, the males and females can easily be differentiated. Males have cobalt rumps and wing and eye markings. Females have emerald green eye markings instead of the blue.

Forpus Conspicillatus / **Spectacled Parrotlet**

The Spectacled Parrotlet is slightly smaller than *F. Coelestis* weighing only 25 to 28 grams or 0.88 to 0.99 ounces. This species is also native to South America and is found in Columbia, Panama, and Venezuela. There are two subspecies of *F. Coelestis*: *Forpus C. Caucae* and *Forpus C. Metae*.

The natural habitats of this species – woodlands and forest – have been severely degraded. As a result, *F. Coelestis* is now listed as at risk. It is therefore very important that you only buy Spectacled Parrotlets from a breeder and not wild caught individuals.

Once adult plumage has emerged it is easy to tell males and females apart. The predominant colour is green with both sexes. Males have violet eye rings while females have emerald green eye rings. Males also have violet on their wings and rumps and the hens have some yellow above their beaks. When these birds first hatch and are still very young their beaks are pink and then turn beige as the individual matures.

These birds are very beautiful, and this combined with their intelligence and big personalities make them increasingly in demand as pets.

Forpus Cyanopygius / **Mexican Parrotlet**

The *F. Cyanopygius* or Mexican Parrotlet comes from – not surprisingly – Mexico. They are spread throughout Western Mexico, the Gulf of Mexico, and across the slopes of the Sierra Madre and have adapted to diverse environments: tropical dry scrubland, subtropical scrublands, and along watercourses. In the wild this species lives in large flocks of up to 50.

Like the Spectacled species, these Parrotlets are predominantly green. Males have multi-tone blue wings and blue rumps. This gives rise to their other names: The Turquoise- or Blue-rumped Parrotlet.

Unlike other species, this one is proving difficult to breed. One reason is that individual birds only breed every one or two years. There are two subspecies: *Forpus C. Pallidus* and *Forpus C. Insularis.*

Forpus Xanthops / **Yellow Faced Parrotlet**

Also known as the Yellow Faced Parrotlet, *F. Xanthops* is among the species found in the pet trade. Small flocks of these birds live on the edges of tropical woodlands in Peru. Like *F. Coelestis* this species faces degraded habitats and is also threatened by poaching.

They are the largest of the *Forpus* genus and are easy to identify thanks to the grey marking on the upper mandible or jaw. The males have violet rumps, blue or cobalt flight feathers (the large feathers in the wings), and grey or blue eye markings.

They are not as easy to keep as some species as they require high humidity levels (80%). Breeding these Parrotlets is also very challenging in part because they mature later and require much larger cages.

These little birds are reputed to be affectionate and easier to handle. However, they are not easy to come by and, because of difficulty breeding them, they are expensive.

Forpus Passerinus / **Green-rumped Parrotlet**

Also known as the Green-rumped Parrotlet, this species is native to north-east Brazil, Columbia, Venezuela, and the island of Trinidad. *F. Passerinus* lives in shrubbery and pastured land. They also make use of abandoned bird's and termite's nests rather than building their own.

The males have grass-green or grey-green colouring on the head and light blues and violet in their wings. This species is the only one where the males don't have blue rumps. The hens are uniform in colour (grass-green) and lack blue feathers, but they have a yellow triangle above the beak.

There are four subspecies of this affectionate Parrotlet: *Forpus P. Cyanophanes/ Cynophanus, Forpus P. Deliciosus, Forpus P. Viridissimus,* and *Forpus P. Cyanochlorus*. Each has slight colour or plumage differences which breeders and hobbyists use to differentiate them.

Forpus Xanthopterygius / **Common / Blue Winged Parrotlet**

This species, also known as the Blue Winged or Common Parrotlet, is indigenous to the south-eastern and central regions of South America. The natural habitats for this species include savannah, scrublands, woodlands, and pastures. These social birds flock in groups of anywhere between 20 and 50.

The male of the species has cobalt feathers in their wings and violet rumps. What makes this species distinctive is the lack of eye markings and larger eye.

The name Common Parrotlet is not apt when it comes to captivity and the pet trade. It is very hard to locate pure *F. Xanthopterygius* or breeders that produce them. In most instances they have been cross-bred with Mexican and Green-rumped Parrotlets. Pure specimens are, in addition to rare, very costly.

This species has no fewer than five distinct subspecies: *Forpus X. Crassirostris, Forpus X. Spengeli, Forpus X. Flavissimus, Forpus X. Flavescens,* and *Forpus X. Olallae*.

The most common species in the pet trade

Of those discussed above, the most popular in the pet trade are:

1. Pacific or Celestial Parrotlet
2. Mexican Parrotlet
3. Spectacled Parrotlet
4. Green rumped Parrotlet

As with other things – including pets unfortunately – the various species move in and out of favour and fashion.

Chapter 3: The Parrotlet as a pet

1) Overview

The Parrotlet has gained rapidly in terms of its popularity as a pet. The main reasons for this are its small size, big personality, beautiful colouring, and quiet voice. If the individual bird is well socialised he or she will make a lovely, affectionate companion that enjoys a cuddle, or at least a head scratch.

They are smart birds, but this is not the species to get if you want a 'talker'. Some Parrotlets do learn a few words or even simple phrases but most don't. The other con with these feathered pets is that they nip and the less well socialised they are the harder and more often they bite!

2) Socialisation & handling

It should be kept in mind when considering getting a bird as a pet that, like exotic or non-traditional pets, they are not the product of hundreds of years of domestication. This means that they require far more time and effort to socialise them than a dog or cat would. They may become aggressive and destructive if not handled often enough.

In addition, they need an environment that matches their natural one as much as possible and – very importantly – allows them to carry out natural, instinctive activities. With Parrotlets these include having space to fly and a habitat that permits foraging.

The failure to provide this is likely to result in a bird that is anxious, shy, not willing to be handled, and that bites or nips far harder and more often than a happier and socialised pet.

It is preferable to obtain a young bird so that it can become used to being handled – and is therefore socialised – from the outset. Socialisation with an older bird that has not had this takes far longer and success is not guaranteed.

As with any socialisation and / or training program, it is essential to reinforce or reward good or desired behaviour. You should not punish bad or undesirable behaviour or the lack of desired behaviour; simply ignore it. The best reinforcers for Parrotlets – and many other pets too – are food in the form of special treats and affection and play.

Socialisation in the form of play, hand feeding, and handling must occur daily so that the bird is happy and remains socialised.

3) One Parrotlet or two?

There is a simple answer to the question of whether you should purchase one or more birds. Unless you plan to have an aviary stocked with a flock of Parrotlets and / or to breed them then you should only get one bird.

The reason for this is that if you have a pair the birds they will understandably bond with each other and neither will need or want affection or time from their owner. While this may suit some, most want a pet that is companionable.

4) Male or female?

Unlike with some pets it makes no difference whether one gets a male or female. How good a pet a bird makes depends entirely on socialisation and has nothing to do with gender.

5) Personality

Owners and breeders of Parrotlets agree when it comes to the range of adjectives they use to describe these pint-sized parrots. They are described as smart, comical, sweet natured, playful, affectionate, fearless, energetic, cheeky, bold, curious, and – if not socialised, handled daily, and given enough attention – they can be aggressive and nippy.

There is danger associated with the fact that they are curious and very active. As an owner you must be constantly aware of where your Parrotlet is as they can be very easily sat or stood on or injured.

While it is necessary to spend time with these little parrots daily, they are also happy to be left on their own if they have an interesting habitat and toys to play with. If they don't they will get bored and may become a little destructive.

6) Behaviour

It can be very helpful to understand what behaviour is normal and what is not. This may inform how you interact with your little feathered friend and help you to realise when he or she is not well.

Feeding behaviour in juvenile Parrotlets

There are a couple of behaviours that may look alarming or worrying but are perfectly normal. They all serve to either protect the young bird or obtain food.

Young birds use vocal calls (chirping) to ask for food. This prompts the parent bird to regurgitate food. Parents also bob their heads to keep the flow of food going.

Defensive behaviour in very young birds that have yet to be weaned involves 'growling' and swaying from side to side. Both are designed to scare away intruders or predators. Both stop once the young bird has been weaned.

Calls

In general terms this species is not noisy at all. They may produce a slightly louder shriek if they are startled or afraid but otherwise the chirps and other calls they make are soft.

Social Noise

Chatting with each other, particularly at dawn and dusk, is an important part of group dynamics in flocks of birds. These calls are necessary for group cohesion and are often accompanied by mutual grooming, which further strengthens bonds within the group.

Pet birds are not truly tame and will continue with their wild or natural activities. You should therefore expect a Parrotlet to be more vocal at these times of day. Given their voices are small these calls are unlikely to bother you and certainly won't cause ructions with neighbours!

Many bird owners find dusk the ideal time to spend social, bonding time with their pet.

Biting

All birds bite, but the less well socialised a bird is the more often it will bite and the more painful it will be for the recipient! Biting by pet birds in an act of self-defence and very rarely aggression. It may also be that a bird is using its beak to hold on or pull itself up rather than biting for biting's sake.

Birds that are used to – and even enjoy – being handled will not be fearful and are therefore unlikely to bite. As you can't punish a pet bird for biting, the solutions are socialisation and training and avoiding the bite.

Owners of Parrotlets that are chronic and severe biters may have to consult a breeder or avian vet for advice on how to handle the problem.

Sleeping Habits

Small birds like this species don't necessarily need a nest box or special perch. As uncomfortable as it may look, they are often quite happy to sleep while holding on to the side bars of a cage or an aviary with their feet and beak.

As tempted as you may be to move a bird to a more comfortable sleeping spot you shouldn't do so as it may not settle again properly that night.

Inappropriate sexual behaviour

Sexually mature birds that have bonded closely with their owner or, conversely, birds that have not been socialised and don't have a suitable mate may exhibit mating behaviour that is abnormal.

In either case, the Parrotlet will attempt to mate with objects such as fingers, hands, toys, or items in the cage or aviary. While this behaviour might appear harmless it should be addressed. The action most often suggested and adopted is the removal of the object that is the target of this behaviour. The second option is obtaining a suitable same-species mate for it.

However, other subtler solutions can be used such as changes to diet, training, and even changes to lighting. A vet or Parrotlet breeder can advise you on the best remedial course to stop and prevent this type of behaviour.

Compulsive or obsessive behaviour

As with some people, individual birds may develop a pattern of behaviour that is habitual, constant, and appears to have no reason or motive. In birds these actions often take the form of rocking, bobbing, or swinging the body or head; pacing; or even spinning or running in circles.

The first step should be to carefully observe the nature and frequency of the behaviour and then take the bird to a vet. Notes on the symptoms, or a video of the behaviour, will assist a vet to make an assessment. It's important to rule out a medical reason for the behaviour. If the problem is not illness or disease it may be that the Parrotlet is bored or unhappy.

The remedy here would be more time with its owner, toys or other objects to play with, or a same-species mate or companion. A more interesting diet helps in some cases too.

7) Parrotlets and other birds

There are some basic facts and simple guidelines when it comes to Parrotlets and other birds.

As previously indicated, these highly social and gregarious small birds need company although they can be left alone quite happily for part of each day. Some breeders state that a single bird needs at least two hours a day with its owner and out of its cage to prevent it becoming lonely and unhappy.

While these little parrots can be kept with a mate or, if the environment is suitable, in a small flock, they should not be kept with birds of a different species. The only exception is budgies, and even then, it may not be a happy combination. You would have to keep an eye on them to make sure they were getting on with each other.

Parrotlets don't know they are very small and will attack birds much larger than themselves. This can have serious consequences for either or both birds. Aggression levels increase at breeding times in both male and female Parrotlets.

8) Parrotlets and other pets

This should go without saying but… a bird should never be out of its cage or left alone if there is a cat or dog in the room or area.

Even domesticated pets still have predatory instincts and one of them is to hunt or at least play with birds. There are bacteria and viruses living naturally in the saliva and under the claws of healthy cats and dogs. These are lethal to birds, so death could result from even a small scratch.

9) *Pocket Parrots & children*

Children can certainly benefit from learning about the responsibility that comes from pet ownership and care. However, birds are not an ideal pet for young children.

Little children are not always aware of their strength and may injure or even crush a tiny bird by accident when 'loving' it. In addition, these pint size birds can bite very hard and will probably do so if handled clumsily or when frightened.

If you have a child or children and a Parrotlet then it is essential to monitor their interactions and teach the child what to do and not do. This could save pain and distress all round!

10) *A word of warning…*

This really does need repeating: these birds are curious, brave, and active. They will walk or fly around when not caged or trained to stay on a perch. You must always know where a Parrotlet is to avoid accidentally stepping or sitting on it or injuring it somehow.

In addition, some birds develop a fascination for shiny or glittery objects, so you must ensure that there aren't any that may pose a choking hazard or that could be damaged by being bitten by a sharp beak. They may even 'borrow' an earring or other small shiny object to play with.

Chapter 4: Buying your Parrotlet

Now it's time to look at choosing the right bird (or birds) to match your lifestyle, taste, environment, and budget.

You also need to be clear about why you are investing in a Parrotlet: will it just be a pet or is breeding them the objective, for instance?

1) How old should a Parrotlet be?

As with all living creatures, birds should not be taken away from their mothers or parents and weaned too young.

The ideal age for weaning varies slightly from one Parrotlet species to the next. For example, Pacific Parrotlets can be weaned slightly earlier than Spectacled Parrotlets.

A good rule of thumb, though, is don't ever buy a bird that is younger than 8 – or at the very least 7 – weeks old.

2) Selecting a Parrotlet breeder

Because some Parrotlet species are under threat in the wild, there are now strict laws governing the importation of these birds and eggs. This added to the growing demand for these pint size birds has meant that there are numerous breeders in the UK, US, and in Europe.

All the reputable breeders go to considerable lengths to ensure that they produce healthy and pure birds. These breeders keep large numbers of birds or work with other breeders to prevent inbreeding and unhealthy cross-breeding to ensure genetic diversity.

This type of breeder will be able to show records tracing their Parrotlet breeding programs and, where there is one available, they will be able to demonstrate membership of a Parrotlet or avian breeders organisation.

If you battle to find a breeder, a local vet, a call or email to a relevant association, an enthusiasts chat room or website, or an Internet search will help.

3) *Choosing an individual bird or birds*

Once the decision is made to get a Parrotlet, the next step is to decide which one to invest in. There are some guidelines which may prove helpful:

- ✓ Decide which species you want. It's fine to be swayed by colour if that's important to you. However, keep in mind that the Pacific or Celestial Parrotlet is thought to be the best option for the beginner and the Yellow faced is more challenging if breeding birds is your aim.

  In addition, not all species and sub-species are available in all countries. For instance, at time of writing the Yellow Faced species was hard to find in the UK.

- ✓ If you are buying a mating or breeding pair, ensure you have a male and female. This may not be easy to be 100% sure of if the birds don't yet have their adult plumage.

- ✓ If you want to breed birds, colour becomes an important consideration for additional and different reasons. The genetics behind this are a little complex but it helps to remember:

  - Pair green, both species and sub-species, with green

  - Pair blue, both species and sub-species, with blue

  - Never pair two red eyed species, as the offspring may be blind.

  If in doubt, check with a breeder, association, or vet.

- ✓ Take the time to observe the bird or birds you like the look of. Just as you would select another type of pet based on its personality, activity level, and so forth you should do this with a bird too. Will he / she / they fit into your family?

✓ While you are observing the bird(s) look out for any indications of illness or injury. Healthy, happy Parrotlets should be active, alert, and bright-eyed. Their colours should be vibrant, and their feathers should be clean and look sleek.

If a bird is breathing strangely, has a runny nose or watery eyes, is sluggish and unresponsive, and / or has clearly lost feathers it is not a healthy bird and should not be purchased.

Chapter 5: What you need to buy & do for your Parrotlet

The diminutive size of Parrotlets does not mean they have small needs. Because they are active they need enough space to fly around and they need interesting cage décor and some toys.

It's important to have the environment set up before you bring your new family member home. While this is not an exhaustive list, it does give an indication of the basic items or supplies you need before you bring your Parrotlet home:

- Suitable foods
- Cage or aviary
- Cage accessories
- Toys
- An avian first aid kit.

Investing in a book or two about Parrotlets is also strongly recommended. The more you know about your bird and what they need the better. It also makes life much easier for you if you have all the information necessary.

1) The cage

Parrotlets have very specific needs when it comes to their environment. They are birds, not helicopters; they need space they can fly around in and cage width is therefore even more important than the height.

General

These little parrots have remarkably strong beaks. This paired with energy and determination means that a cage needs to have strong bars. They shouldn't be thin enough for your pet to bend the bars or dismantle the cage. Apart from the risk that a bird could escape, if it got caught in a hole it could be severely injured or even die.

Experts also recommend a flat roofed cage as opposed to one with a domed or vaulted roof. This shape of cage makes it easier for the occupants to grip the bars and for you to hang toys from the roof and to position perches of various kinds.

Other factors to keep in mind is that the cage must be easy to clean, allow access to change toys and remove items for cleaning or filling, have multiple doors (a minimum of three), and be made of safe and non-toxic materials.

Cage size

The advice from breeders and owners alike when it comes to cage size is, "As big as the space allows!" This is especially the case for birds that will be caged for most of each day.

The optimal type of cage is a flight cage, which is ideal for active, lively birds such as Parrotlets. As previously mentioned, the cage must be wider than it is tall so that there is room to fly. Flight cages are, as a rule, 32 by 35 centimetres or 12.6 by 13.8 inches in dimension. However, many breeders strongly suggest a minimum size of by 46 by 61 centimetres or 18 by 24 inches.

The width between the bars is also significant as these small birds can get their heads stuck if the gap is too wide. It is recommended that the bars should be ½ inch or 13 millimetres apart.

The bottom of the cage is also a feature that should be considered for your sake and that of the cage occupants. Some breeders and hobbyists are not in favour of grated bottoms, as they believe it is not good for the bird's feet. However, very little time is spent on the cage floor generally and the bars will make it easier for gripping. A pull-out tray below the floor that collects fallen food and debris and droppings makes cleaning the cage easier.

Finally, the doors in the cage should include two feed doors – one for food and one for water – and another main door that is big enough for your hand to fit through.

2) Cage accessories

There are several items that are necessary in a Parrotlet's cage. Most of them are for the benefit of your brightly coloured pet but some make your life easier too.

> *Perches*: Most cages come with dowels; get rid of them and replace them with perches of suitable material and in the right location. Often placing perches at either side of the cage will encourage birds to fly the length of the cage and they will have an unobstructed flight path.

There is no need for expensive perches. The best ones are made of small branches or clean, natural wood. So long as the material is safe for Parrotlets, it can be fun for the bird to be given a branch complete with a few leaves.

Some owners use apple, rowan, willow, ash, hazel, citrus trees, eucalyptus, pine, hawthorn, balsa, or even bamboo branches. Natural branches are also good to chew, not only to perch on. It is vital, though, that the branches you use are clean and free of droppings, insecticide, or pesticide.

It's also important to select branches / perches of varying diameters. These should range from ½ to 1 inch or 1.3 to 2.5 centimetres. This variation helps to prevent problems with the bird's feet and exercises the foot muscles. One can also buy a pedi-perch from bird supply shops, which prevent nails becoming too long.

Don't place perches above food or water containers because they are likely to become contaminated with droppings or use store bought perches that are covered with sandpaper, as they will hurt your bird's feet.

> *Food and water bowls*: Parrotlets don't like using covered food and water bowls so select open ones. It's a good idea to buy four bowels so that you have a clean set in reserve.

There is some debate about where dishes should be placed. Some owners say put the bowls next to each other while others say place them at opposite ends of the cage to encourage the bird to fly between them and to reduce the chance of the water becoming contaminated with food.

It's probably best to experiment by moving them around to see what works for your pet and you. In addition, placing food too close to perches may result in overeating and damage to the food bowls if the bird decides it's also a chew toy.

➢ *Toys*: These are very important for smart, active, playful birds like Parrotlets to prevent them becoming bored, unhappy, and potentially destructive.

The first consideration when looking at toys is the safety of the bird. Avoid toys that have metal unless it is stainless steel, as it won't rust or flake. Items that include materials such as cotton that are made from fine fibres are also unsafe as the fibres may be swallowed and, over time, will build up in the digestive system and lead to death.

There is a wide range of toys for birds available. However, you should get ones designed for small and medium sized birds. Popular choices include chew toys (made from wood, leather, small pinecones, or cuttlefish), ladders, boings, swings, ropes, hoops, bells, and puzzle toys. Mirrors are not a good idea, especially for single birds, as they may bond with their reflection and not their owner!

You should place enough toys in the cage that the bird can play, but not so many they restrict flight paths or become a source of stress. It can work well to hang one or two from the roof of the cage. If your bird doesn't play with them they can be relocated. In addition, it's necessary to change half the toys about once a week to prevent boredom and keep your feathered pet's life interesting.

➢ *Cage substrate*: Many owners think that paper – even newspaper – is a good material to place on the bottom of the cage. Paper of some kind also allows one to monitor the number and appearance of droppings too; these can be an indication of health or illness in a pet bird.

It is also easier to replace this type of floor covering than materials such as wood shavings, which can harbour mould, bacteria and / or fungus. Your pet should never come into direct contact with the substrate because it is not hygienic.

Regardless of the substrate selected, the cage floor must be cleaned weekly as small birds can become ill very quickly from bacteria in their environment. You can either use purpose-made cleaning agents or neat or diluted white vinegar for this purpose.

➤ *Security*: Even happy and healthy birds will at some point feel the need for privacy and peace and quiet. Place something in the cage that your Parrotlet can retreat into to feel safe. One can use a small box or even a paper bag.

3) Cage location

The cage should be somewhere warm but not in direct sun. If you live in a warm climate and you have an outdoors aviary you must ensure that the birds have somewhere to stay cool or warm up. Provide a shaded area or some sort of structure in the cage for this purpose.

Similarly, positions where there are draughts must be avoided or there must be areas the cage occupants can go to get out of the breeze. Don't place cages near air-conditioning units or the air flow from them.

Your Parrotlet is a curious and social creature. It will probably enjoy having its cage where it is close to you or family activity so that it can watch what is going on and be 'involved'. It makes it easier to chat to your bird too, which will help to improve bonding and socialisation levels.

4) Sleep and rest time

Parrotlets need a lot of sleep as they expend a great deal of energy when they are awake. Many breeders say that one should allow these little birds to have around 12 hours of sleep at night.

To have an undisturbed night they need darkness, preferably between the same hours each day. A cage should be covered with a cloth that keeps out the light but does not restrict air flow.

An outside, large cage or aviary that can't be covered should be constructed or placed in area that is protected from light.

If you have multiple cages the birds in them can find seeing each other and the movement disturbing, even stressful. To avoid this, place a barrier of some sort between them: a screen, piece of fabric, or a plant.

5) Play time

Wild Parrotlets spend their waking hours foraging for food and flying around. They also have the members of their flock to socialise with.

A captive bird needs its owner to provide food, exercise, and – very importantly – play and social time outside the cage for two to four hours a day.

You need to use common sense to safeguard your Parrotlet *and* the things in your home that you want to protect. Your pet bird needs a safe area in which to stretch its wings and legs and spend time with you. These things are vital for physical and emotional well-being.

Chapter 6: Introducing your Parrotlet to its new home

As with any new pet you introduce into your home, there are things that should be done (and not done) to make the adjustment a happy and successful one for all concerned.

1) Settling in

Arriving in a new environment is stressful for all creatures and your new Parrotlet(s) will be no exception.

A newly arrived single bird

Regardless of the age of your new feathery pet it will need time to acclimatise and settle into its new home and to get used to you and any other family members. Some individuals settle quickly whereas others may take a few days.

The best approach is to place the new arrival into its cage and just leave it in peace for a couple of hours to calm down and start looking around. Make sure there is food and water available. It can be very helpful to provide some treats, such as millet, that your new bird will find irresistible, as this should encourage it to start eating.

Once your pet is settled, you'll need to 'wean' it off treat foods onto more nutritious ones. A helpful strategy is to put only healthy food out in the morning because that is when your bird will be hungry.

After the initial period of adjustment spent quietly on its own, it's time for you to introduce yourself to your new family member. At this point it's too soon to handle the Parrotlet; you need to sit next to the cage and talk quietly. Offering the new arrival treats will also make introductions go more smoothly and get your bird used to being near your hand and fingers.

Some individuals will adjust in a matter of a day or two, while others will feel anxious for longer. Don't force matters and take your lead from him or her. Once a Parrotlet is feeling settled and confident it will play with its toys and be prepared to step up onto your hand.

You will be able to take it out of its cage too (as long as the room is safe) as long as you are willing and able to retrieve it from whatever perch it decides to use. Being able to call your bird so that it comes to you will make your life easier in this regard.

Settling in a pair

The golden rule in this situation is to introduce the pair to each other in a neutral cage or area. Parrotlets are territorial and if a new bird is introduced into an established territory or cage the two birds may well fight. These fights can be very violent, particularly if either bird is ready to mate, and may result in serious injury or even death.

A sure sign that your birds have formed a bonded pair is not only the absence of fights. Bonded birds will usually sit side by side.

Introducing a Parrotlet into a home with other birds

As with any other type of pet, it is very important to keep the new arrival separate from other birds for 30 days. This is in effect a quarantine period that will safeguard the health of all your birds.

In addition to keeping them apart, it is necessary to practise good hygiene by using different water and food bowls and washing your hands thoroughly before and after working with both new and existing birds.

It is also highly recommended that you take your new bird or birds to a vet who can make sure that all is as it should be and answer any questions you may have.

2) Socialising / taming your Parrotlet

Socialising domesticated pets is important and especially so with those that are still wild, like birds. Given how crucial it is, it is good news that these little parrots are not difficult to work with. The sooner you start interacting with your pet – talking to it, offering it treats, handling it, etcetera – the easier it will be to tame your Parrotlet and keep it that way.

As with any other pet, you need to become familiar with what your bird does and doesn't enjoy. A little nip is a sure sign that it's not enjoying something or has had enough!

3) Hand taming a baby bird

This is only an option if one owns a breeding pair that have produced young. It is a practise used by breeders so that they have young birds that are already socialised.

Hand taming is not the same as hand rearing. With hand rearing one feeds baby birds who have lost or been taken away from their parents after a couple of weeks. Hand taming involves young that are being fed / reared by their parents but are removed and handled each day. This type of rearing has two significant advantages.

Firstly, the baby bird is receiving food from its parents for the first three weeks of its life as it would in the wild. It is fed on the perfect diet. The mother produces crop milk and the father feeds the mother digested food, which mixes with the milk in the mother's crop. This highly nutritious mixture is fed to the baby and promotes health and growth.

Secondly, beginning the taming and socialisation process when a Parrotlet is still at such a young age results in far tamer, happier, and more relaxed pet birds. This has advantages for both the bird and the owner.

Once the baby is about 2 weeks old, remove it from its parents each day for a very short period. Given babies are easily startled and their eyes are not fully developed or open, it is very important that the handling session takes place somewhere quiet and dimly lit. After 3 weeks the handling sessions can increase to twice daily and last a little longer. The baby must be returned to the parents after each session.

If you are gentle, consistent in the hand taming, speak softly, and return the baby to mum and dad, it will start to trust you and become tamer within days.

Some parents may have other ideas. More protective parents will not be at all happy to let you remove a baby from their care. If this occurs, don't force the issue and try again when the babies are a little older.

As the young bird matures you can begin training it too. It is very helpful if your bird learns to 'step up' and 'step down' or move onto or off your hand or finger.

Chapter 7: Training your pet Parrotlet

There are three things to remember when you are training a Parrotlet: be very patient; use rewards and never punishment; and be prepared for the fact that it may not work.

This is especially true of teaching your bird to talk. Although this is an intelligent species they are not great talkers, particularly the females.

The basics should be taught before you attempt teaching your feathered pupil to talk or do tricks. The main training is 'step up', 'step down', and recall. Talking is only for your benefit but doing tricks can help to keep a captive bird stimulated and entertained.

1) How to train your feathered pet

The use of positive reinforcement is essential. In other words, negative or undesirable behaviour should be ignored, and positive or desired behaviour must be rewarded immediately.

One can never punish a bird. The way to attempt to end or change negative behaviour is to ignore your pet or put it down. Being deprived of your company and interaction with you will be punishment enough.

Rewards should involve vocal reinforcement ("Good bird", "Clever bird" and so on) and – most importantly – a treat. Once you have established the food your Parrotlet enjoys the most you should use it as the reward for good behaviour and not include it in the usual diet.

Training sessions must be held several times a day and should not last too long or the bird may become tired, stressed, and / or bored. Some breeders suggest one or two sessions a day each lasting 10 to 15 minutes.

2) Step-up, step down training

Your Parrotlet needs to work up to being able to get onto and off your finger or hand when you ask it to. Unless the breeder has already done this training, it is the first thing your new bird should be taught.

Begin by placing your hand inside the cage. Remember not to make any sudden movements that may frighten your pet or be seen by it as threatening. Don't attempt to get too close to your Parrotlet initially either.

Once you have had your hand in the cage a few times a day for short periods for several days, progress to moving your hand closer to the bird. Do so while also offering it some irresistible snack. You want your hand to be associated with something pleasant and enjoyable.

Place your hand next to the bird. Tempt your Parrotlet to step up onto or into your hand. As you do so say "Step up". Once he or she is on your hand or finger provide a reward. This must be continued until your pet responds to the verbal command.

The same applies to "step down" but instead of placing your hand next to the bird, you do so next to a perch or the bottom of the cage. The verbal command must be given, and a reward must be provided when the pupil gets it right.

Being able to ask your bird to step up and down will make it much easier for you to take it out of the cage for social, bonding, and play times or if you need to provide medical care.

3) Recall training

You will need and want to be able to call your bird to you. Apart from other considerations, this is preferable to having to climb onto furniture or up a ladder to retrieve a bird that has settled on a ceiling light or curtain rail!

As with all other training, it needs to be done in small increments and regularly. Begin by placing your hand or finger within hopping distance of your pet. Place a treat next to your finger and call your Parrotlet. When it hops onto your finger provide a treat and praise.

Over time you should move your hand or finger further and further away from your pet so that he or she must travel further to reach you. Each time you call your bird and he or she comes to you lavish it with praise and hand over the reward.

The same technique can be used to train your pet to sit on a perch outside the cage or on your shoulder. Touch the stand or your shoulder, have the training treat in your other hand, and call the bird to you. When it responds you must reward it as you usually do.

4) Stopping a bird from nipping

As with most parrot species, Parrotlets can be nippy. Despite the small size of their beaks a nip can be most painful. The urge to bite is a natural one and more likely if a bird is feeling threatened, unwell, or just plain grumpy.

Pet birds need to be trained not to nip and – as with other training – the sooner one starts the better. Baby birds are more likely to nibble a finger than give a sore bite. However, nibbling should also be discouraged, as it can be the precursor to biting when the bird is older.

With babies it is relatively easy to stop nibbling. You could give them something to play with or chew on other than your finger such as a toy or a piece of cardboard. Another option is to very gently push against the beak / into the bite. This second option should be reinforced by saying "No" and putting the bird down. As with other negative behaviour, ignore your Parrotlet for a few minutes.

5) *Talking*

If someone tells you that these tiny parrots are great talkers and will develop large vocabularies don't believe them! Unlike other parrots, Parrotlets are not great talkers. They are more on a par with cockatiels in this respect. However, if you want to try, you can begin training when your bird is about 3 months old.

The best one can hope for – and it's more likely with a well-trained male bird than a female – is in the region of a dozen words and a short tune or two that they will 'whistle'.

As with other bird species, speech is mimicry and not talking. Birds also are better at repeating single words; phrases – even short ones – are hard for Parrotlets to learn.

Some owners say that birds learn to talk in part by lip reading. This may not be the case at all but there's no harm in looking directly at your pet when you try to teach it to speak or mimic human speech. What is true is that a great deal of repetition is required; even then, most Parrotlets – especially females – will not learn to speak.

Finally, given this species has a soft call they sound as though they are whispering when they do talk. If vocal ability is what you want in an avian pet, then a Parrotlet is not a good choice for you.

6) *Final thoughts*

For both stopping undesirable behaviour such as biting and initiating good behaviour like stepping up:

- Don't place your bird in a situation which may provoke bad behaviour. For instance, don't frighten or make it feel cornered or it probably will bite. That would be your fault, not his.

- Be patient and don't do too much too soon. A pet won't come to you if they have not even got used to you or mastered stepping up and down.

- Only use brief withdrawal of interaction as punishment. There should never be any actions that would either frighten or hurt a pet.

- Use food and verbal praise to reward and reinforce good behaviour. If your Parrotlet enjoys having its head stroked that can form part of the reward too.

- Start training early and make training sessions both regular and brief. Even after something is learned it needs to be repeated and reinforced so it is not forgotten.

Chapter 8: Caring for your Parrotlet

As an owner one is responsible for meeting all the needs of one's pet. These are both physical and emotional.

To fulfil this duty when it comes to Parrotlets, it is necessary to reproduce their natural habitat as closely as possible while also making up for the things that one probably can't provide such as being part of a social group or flock.

1) Environmental requirements

There are a few factors that should be kept in mind when it comes to the physical environment you will keep your pet in.

- *Temperature*: Fortunately, Parrotlets cope with a broad range of temperatures. A good rule of thumb is that if the temperature is comfortable for you it will also be fine for your feathered friend.

  However, any marked change to temperature should be introduced slowly so the bird can acclimatise. If the temperature becomes much colder quickly it is essential to cover the cage with a blanket. Healthy birds cope with temperature changes far better than sick ones.

- *Light*: These little parrots enjoy sunlight but, as stated earlier, they should not be left in direct sunlight unless there is a shaded, cooler area they can move to if they feel too hot.

  They need darkness or near darkness to sleep properly so either the cage must to covered or it should be in a room or area that is not used at night.

- *Humidity*: Again, Parrotlets are adaptable little creatures and are not too demanding as far as air moisture levels are concerned. Given they are often native to more subtropical locations, some species may be a little happier in a slightly more humid environment.

If you are told by the breeder or your vet that this applies to your pet, you can try spraying it from time to time with water from a bottle that produces a fine mist. Putting the cage in the bathroom is also an option but not if it gets too hot.

2) Regular care & hygiene

Captive birds that are kept indoors require more care in terms of their feathers, nails, beaks, and feet than wild or outdoor ones do. This is particularly true of individuals that are fed a pure seed diet. There are several things that should be done regularly to ensure the well-being and health of your pet.

Grooming and bathing

You won't need to groom your Parrotlet as they are clean little creatures and self-groom. However, these little birds enjoy bathing every day.

If space doesn't allow for a bowl for bathing in, some owners provide wet foliage (soft leaves such as spinach and lettuce leaves work well). If your bird shows no signs of wanting to bathe you can encourage him or her to groom itself by spraying it lightly with clean water.

Part of natural grooming involves picking at new feathers. As a feather emerges the pin or sheath must be picked at to open and remove the pin and open the new feather. This is healthy and not to be confused with abnormal behaviour such as excessive feather picking or a health problem such as the presence of mites.

If your Parrotlet somehow gets dirty, and it's a substance like oil that it can't or shouldn't deal with on its own, you can use a very mild cleaning agent such as baby shampoo. After cleaning its feathers, you should rinse and dry them.

Wing clipping

Some websites, owners, and even breeders recommend clipping pet bird's wings. This is, however, generally thought to be bad advice.

These active little birds *need* to be able to fly. It's very important both in terms of their physical health and their happiness.

Banding

Most breeders band the birds they raise. It helps them to trace breeding lines and to identify birds. You can either remove the band or leave it on. The decisions may be informed by whether you intend to breed Parrotlets.

If you leave a leg band – particularly a closed one – in place you need to check under it and the leg regularly. If there are any signs of swelling or constriction a vet will have to remove the band. Dirt can also accumulate under a band, which may cause sores or even infection.

Cage care and hygiene

Cleaning the cage daily serves two important purposes:

- ✓ It will prevent your pet from developing certain illnesses that result from spoilt food or contaminated water.

- ✓ It can alert you to the fact that your Parrotlet is not well, as you will notice changes in faecal matter and urine such as the presence of blood or changes in frequency, consistency, or colour.

Water and food bowls must be thoroughly cleaned every day. Don't clean them in the same place you wash dishes used by you and others as contamination can occur. Preferably don't wash pet dishes or accessories in your kitchen but rather do so outside.

If at some point you notice that there is faecal matter, food, or any other foreign matter in the water bowl, the water should be replaced as soon as possible.

There are several options when it comes to cleaning agents that will deal with dried droppings and other substances in the cage. You can use dish soap (not the same bottle you use of the family dishes, though) to clean the cage and perches. Remember to rinse surfaces well with clean water and dry them afterwards.

You can disinfect the various surfaces with diluted bleach or white vinegar. Alternatively, pet stores sell a disinfectant that is specially formulated for use in bird cages. As with cleaning, you must rinse and dry the surfaces thoroughly afterwards. You don't want to expose your pet to chemicals.

When cleaning the cage, you need to safeguard your health too. It is recommended that you wear disposable gloves when you clean the cage. Dispose of them after use and, even if your hands were covered, wash them very thoroughly with warm water and soap.

3) Toxic plants

It was stated earlier that using natural, hardwood branches as perches works very well. Some owners make use of fresh branches complete with leaves and even berries. While this is an excellent idea you must ensure that you don't accidentally use a plant that is toxic.

Trees and shrubs that must be avoided include: mountain laurel, ficus, red maple, nectarine trees, flame tree, rhododendron, rubber plant, oak tree, sandbox tree, bleeding heart holly, oleander schefflera, boxwood, peach tree, hydrangea, philodendron, plum tree, Jerusalem cherry tree, poinsettia, oak, cherry tree, may apple tree, chestnut tree, mistletoe, privet hedge, eucalyptus, prune trees, white cedar, and yews.

Other plants that must not be in the environment where your pet could nibble on them include: amaryllis, euonymus, purple sea bane, andromeda, felt plant, mushrooms, ranunculi, narcissus, rhubarb, bean plant, bird of paradise, foxglove, nutmeg, salvia, heliotrope, schefflera, honeysuckle, flowers from bulbs, hyacinth, peony, buttercup, periwinkle, snowdrop, bracken, fern, iris, sorrel, ivy, calla lily, jasmine, poinsettia, marigold, poppy, dieffenbachia, potato plants, tomato plants, elderberry, mock orange, elephant ear monkshood, and umbrella plant.

Please note that these lists are not exhaustive. If unsure, please check with an avian vet, Parrotlet breeder or specialist pet store.

4) Household threats & dangers

There are many things that you have and do in your home that could put your little bird in harm's way.

Air-borne toxins

For instance, many air-borne substances can damage a bird's respiratory system, sometimes fatally. Cigarette and other smoke, air fresheners and the fumes released by candles, incense sticks, spray deodorants and household cleaners are bad for birds. Even self-cleaning ovens and non-stick cookware may release fumes when heated.

Accidental injury

You must be vigilant when your pet is out of its cage; make sure you or a responsible person always know where he or she is.

There are many horror stories of loving owners accidentally putting something on top of their bird, not noticing that it had gone into a cupboard or appliance or standing on a pet as it wandered around on the floor. It can happen all too easily given their size and the fact that they are quiet. Bird bones are brittle and even a casually tossed cushion could have tragic consequences.

Appliances

For the periods when your Parrotlet will be flying free in the house you must ensure that ceiling fans are off and that there are no hot surfaces or pots, pans etcetera that your bird might touch.

Don't leave the doors of large appliances such as microwaves, fridges, freezers, washing machines or tumble-dryers open. If you do, check very carefully that your little pet is not inside before closing the door or using the appliance.

Windows and mirrors

It should go without saying that windows should all be closed when a bird is out of its cage.

Windows and mirrors both pose a risk as a Parrotlet will not realise the glass is there and will also mistake the reflection in a mirror for an open area. In both cases there is a danger that he or she will fly into the mirror or glass and be injured. A bird flying fast enough may even break its neck.

You could place decals or strips of tape over windows and mirrors by many owners find that impractical and unappealing. A further solution is to cover mirrors with a cloth and draw the curtains until your pet is back in its cage. If closed curtains make an interior too dull, fine net curtains might be a good option.

Chapter 9: Feeding your Parrotlet

1) Feeding in the wild

Parrotlets in the wild eat a mixture of foods that provide all the nutrients that they require. They feed on various fruits and berries, nuts, seeds and seed heads and even blossoms. Captive birds need the same nutrition and it's their owner's responsibility to make sure they receive it.

These birds are very active, and they also have fast metabolisms. These two factors mean that, despite their small size, they need to eat a lot and regularly.

2) What to feed your Parrotlet

Pet Parrotlets may not have access to the foods their wild counterparts do, but they can still have a varied and interesting diet. A pure seed menu is not ideal for these birds.

There are now foods specifically formulated to meet the needs of this species. These pellets would be sufficient but on their own they would constitute a very boring diet for birds that enjoy variety. You should also give your pint-sized parrot a selection of fruit and vegetables.

Include some seeds such as millet, fruit such as apple, mango, cherries, peaches, pears, melons, grapes, kiwi fruit and rowan and hawthorn berries. Good vegetables include peas, spinach, dried or cooked (and well rinsed) lentils, carrots, kale, broccoli and sweet or bell peppers. These foods must be cut into small pieces. This allows your Parrotlet to hold it with its feet and manipulate it as it eats.

Some breeders also use defrosted frozen and mixed vegetables and sprouted lentils and mung beans in addition to fresh or cooked and cooled vegetables such as sweet potato, brown rice, and corn. Cooked egg is sometimes also given to birds.

Calcium and vitamins A and D are important. Vitamin A is found in orange and dark green vegetables, but the other vitamins and minerals are easier to supply in the form of a supplement for small birds. These are readily available at specialty pet stores or from a vet. Cuttlefish can also be a useful source of calcium.

It is important not to give your Parrotlet too many sunflower seeds or a lot of protein. Keep sunflower seeds to a minimum. Too much protein can precipitate an unseasonal breeding condition, which can lead to health problems. Some breeders state that seeds are better if they have been soaked or even germinated rather than just dry. It is, however, crucial not to leave them longer than 24 hours or they become mouldy.

Regardless of what food you opt for and how you prepare it, it is essential to ensure that your Parrotlet has a balanced and nutritional diet to prevent him or her developing health problems. You may also find it helpful to increase the quantity of food when your bird is moulting or breeding and therefore has increased nutritional needs.

If you are unsure about diet, consult your vet or the breeder you purchased your Parrotlet from.

Keep in mind that high quality diets also strengthen the immune system allowing your Parrotlet to resist infections far more easily.

3) *Diet in breeding birds*

Diet is always important but laying hens have additional requirements to keep them and the eggs healthy and strong. The primary reason for this is the female loses a great deal of calcium because the mineral is used to produce the eggs.

Although cuttlefish provides calcium, breeders recommend that you use a special food mix formulated for breeding female birds. This feed meets their requirements before, during, and after laying. You can start giving her the mix a few times a week when she is showing signs of being broody and before she lays her eggs. Once the babies hatch the special feed should be given to her every day to replenish the minerals and fats that she lost during the breeding and laying process and while feeding the babies.

4) *Water and your Parrotlet*

It is necessary to make sure that your bird has constant access to fresh, clean water. Water bowls must be cleaned each day. If your pet is fond of bathing you need a second dish for him or her to splash around in.

Water bowls should never be placed under perches as this increases the likelihood that the water will be contaminated by droppings.

5) *What NOT to feed your Parrotlet*

There are many things that are bad for your Parrotlet, just as there are for pets such as domestic dogs and cats. These guidelines and rules should help you avoid unhealthy or toxic foodstuffs and keep your pet healthy.

While you might not deliberately feed any of these foodstuffs to your feathered family member, they may encounter and eat some, perhaps without you even realising it. You need to exercise care about leaving foodstuffs where they are accessible.

While *not* a comprehensive list, the following foods are potentially lethal for your bird: foods high in fat, sugar, or salt; alcohol; tobacco; caffeine; carbonated drinks; dried fruits that contain either sulphates or sulphides; milk or cream; apricot, nectarine, cherry, peach, and plum pips; apple and pear seeds; peanuts; citrus fruit; lima, kidney, and dried beans; chocolate; olives; raw and cooked onion and garlic; asparagus; avocado; butter; parsley; tomato; egg plant; potato; and rhubarb.

Chapter 10: Health management

Parrotlets are a hardy species of bird and rarely become ill if they are properly fed and housed. However, no matter how robust a species or individual creature is, it is not immune to illness. Injuries can happen too, particularly with Parrotlets as they are active and very small and – like all birds – have very fragile bones.

Something to keep in mind when choosing a pet is that birds with colour mutations – especially the rarer ones – are more prone to health problems. It is thought that this may be the result of a gene pool that is not yet sufficiently diverse.

Many of the health issues Parrotlets are susceptible to are the same ones that other birds, especially parrots, fall victim to.

1) Choosing a vet

Don't wait until your little bird is ill or hurt to find a vet. As soon as your Parrotlet comes home with you it's important to locate an avian vet in your area or at least a vet practice that regularly treats birds. You can ask local bird clubs, the breeder you bought your pet from, or a regional or national bird association for details or recommendations.

In addition to treating your Parrotlet, if it gets sick or injured a vet can advise you on various routine preventative measures to keep your pet as healthy as possible.

While they are a new development, vaccinations are now available for birds. An avian vet will be able to advise you about vaccinations for your bird: which ones might be necessary, how often they are needed and risks – if any – associated with them.

2) A vet examination for a new bird

When you take your Parrotlet to the vet for the first time it will undergo a very thorough examination. This should ideally be done within the first three or four days after you bring your bird home. The earlier health problems are spotted the better.

The vet will determine whether your pet is healthy and, if it is, the examination results provide base readings that will help determine the bird's state of health in the future. This initial examination is comprehensive and includes:

✓ *Weight measurement*: This is measured in grams not ounces as this is more accurate at low weights such as these and is better able to detect even small fluctuations in body mass.

Once a bird has reached adulthood its weight should be constant. Any changes in its weight can provide important indications of feeding or health issues or problems. While you can weigh your bird at home, it will be weighed at its annual exam and during any other vet visits.

✓ *Medical history*: The vet will ask for information about your bird: age, how long you have had it, where you bought it, what environment you keep it in, its diet, contact with other birds, and where you buy the food you give it.

Importantly, the vet will ask you why you are concerned about your Parrotlet. This is the time to mention any behavioural differences, changes to droppings and so on that you have noticed and been worried about.

✓ *Physical examination:* While you will pick up on many changes in your bird such as laboured breathing, lassitude, runny eyes for example, a skilled avian vet will establish even more through a hands-on physical examination.

These professionals will pick up abnormalities in a bird's feet, beak, feathers, eyes, tongue, ears, skin, nostrils (nares), muscles, bones and abdomen.

Depending on what the vet finds during the physical examination and is told by you, he or she may decide further assessment and testing is necessary. These may include some, or all, of the following:

▪ *Examination of droppings*: Because your bird won't produce faeces or urine to order it's a good idea to take some samples with you. You could remove the substrate from the cage, place it carefully in a bag, seal the bag and take it with you.

To a vet's trained eye, the characteristics of droppings (composition, colour, and volume) can say a great deal about a bird's state of health or assist with making a diagnosis.

Faecal matter may also be examined under a microscope, as this will detect the presence of internal parasites.

- *Parrot Fever (Chlamydophila) test*: This disease used to be called *Psittacosis*. The screening test – and there are several types available – will be part of your Parrotlet's initial and annual exam because this very nasty bacterium not only poses a grave health risk to birds but also to you.

- *Blood tests*: A standard blood test looks at the number of white and red blood cells. These counts can also help to identify deficiencies or illness.

  The test also looks for any chemical imbalances that may indicate organ disease. Finally, blood tests can also identify blood-borne parasites.

- *X-rays / radiography*: These tests have a far wider application than looking for broken or damaged bones. They can also show lumps, masses such as tumours, foreign objects, and the health or otherwise of the lungs.

- *Microbiology / bacterial cultures*: If the vet suspects that there is a bacterial infection present, he or she may take fluid or tissue samples to (a) look for the presence of bacteria or yeast, (b) identify any bacteria or yeast, and (c) test if the feathered patient is sensitive to certain antibiotics so they can be avoided. Samples for testing might be taken from more than one site and could include the throat, genital area, or crop (oesophagus).

- *Cytology / viral cultures*: These tests look for the presence of viruses rather than bacteria. While antibiotics can't treat viral infections, once a virus has been identified it can be managed and the bird given symptomatic relief.

It is certainly not the case that all these tests will be done each time your Parrotlet visits a vet. The history taking, weighing, and examination will be regular features.

However, more sophisticated tests are only necessary if your bird is injured or sick or the vet suspects that there is a problem.

3) *Moulting versus abnormal feather loss*

All birds moult and this annual loss of feathers is normal. With Parrotlets, the first moult usually takes place at around 4 or 5 months. Moulting may make your pet a little grumpy or even aggressive for a day or two.

Usually all feathers, including tail and wing feathers, are shed and then replaced just before breeding season. Not all feathers are shed at the same time, as enough feathers must be retained to make flight possible and to keep the bird at a regular temperature. Baldness or even bald patches are a sign of abnormal feather loss.

If your Parrotlet has bald patches, then it's necessary to find out why and to treat the underlying cause. There can be many reasons why feathers fall out or why the bird itself will pick or pull out its feathers. Because the reasons for abnormal feather loss are varied and can mimic each other it is usually necessary to involve an avian vet so he or she can make an accurate diagnosis. Some possibilities are:

> *Psittacine and Polyomavirus (Feather and Beak disease)*: These are serious viral illnesses that can cause feather loss or at least damage. While the viruses can be detected, treatment is rarely successful because feather loss as a symptom usually means that the disease is advanced and that the infected bird will die.

> Avian vaccines are being developed so it is worth asking your vet about any that may help to protect your pet against these viruses.

> *Parasite infestation: Knemidokoptes*, also known as "scaly face and legs", is a skin parasite that is not uncommon in pet birds. It causes the tissue on the legs and face to thicken and this change is visible to the naked eye. However, vets often confirm the diagnosis by doing tests. It's also preferable to consult a vet as some over-the-counter remedies can cause more harm than good.

52

The second group of surface parasites that cause irritation to the skin and can lead to feather loss are lice and both feather and red mites.

Finally, a protozoan (a minute worm) parasite called *Giardia* that lives in the intestine can, bizarrely, cause the infested bird to pull out its feathers. This parasite can only be accurately diagnosed through examination under a microscope of droppings.

➢ *Bacterial and fungal diseases:* Skin irritation can also be the result of bacteria and fungi, specifically *Pseudomonas* and *Staphylococcus* bacteria. Feather loss is a result of the bird scratching excessively or pulling its feathers to relieve the itching and pain. The primary fungal culprits are *Aspergillus* and *Candidiasis*.

With both bacteria and fungi, a definitive diagnosis can't be made without first taking tissue samples and doing cultures.

➢ *Nutritional deficiencies:* The two dietary problems that can lead to feather loss are a vitamin A deficiency or a severe lack of protein. The best course of action would be to tell the vet what your bird currently eats and ask for advice on changes to the diet.

➢ *Behavioural causes:* Most of the self-injurious behaviour, including pulling out its own feathers, is a result of unhappiness, frustration, or boredom. A captive bird has no real substitute for its natural environment and social structure. It has no flock to belong to and interact with, many have no mate, and they have hormonally-driven mating, breeding, and nesting drives and no way to express them.

Even the most loving owner who has bonded with their Parrotlet is not an adequate substitute for other birds of the same species. Unfortunately, these feelings can be channelled into obsessive and destructive self-mutilation which may result in both feather and skin damage.

The only ways to try and deal with this destructive and unhealthy behaviour are to consider obtaining a mate for a single bird, ensure you spend time with your pet, and provide ample toys, including foraging toys, which are changed regularly to provide variety.

> *Cage mate aggression:* Sometimes these little birds don't get on as well with the other occupants of the cage as one would like. There are situations in which an individual bird is repeatedly attacked or bullied by another.

If a bird is being attacked by another and losing feathers or being injured as a result, the victim should be removed and kept in a separate area until the lost feathers have a chance to regrow.

If the aggressor is not actually pulling out the feathers but is causing so much stress that feathers are falling out, you will have to separate the birds permanently.

> *Other causes:* Stress, injury, and exposure to toxins and irritants such as fumes or smoke can lead to feather picking.

There are also some diseases that cause stress and / or feather picking. These include cysts, tumours, and illnesses that affect the respiratory and gastrointestinal systems or the liver or kidneys.

4) Common Parrotlet illnesses and health problems

It can be hard to work out that your Parrotlet is ill. One reason is that these birds will often continue to eat and drink when they are ill. This is a natural, instinctive defence called "masking" and it is designed to hide illness and weakness from predators.

This means that often by the time signs of illness are clear the bird has been ill for some time and, with more serious conditions, it may be too late to save it. The only way to try and prevent this is by becoming truly familiar with your Parrotlet's appearance and behaviour and by monitoring how much it's eating and checking its droppings when you change the substrate each day.

A further complicating factor is that many of the illnesses that avian pets may contract have the same or similar symptoms. This has given rise to the term "sick-bird syndrome". Only a vet will be able to make a specific diagnosis. However, there are some signs and indications you should watch for.

Common signs of illness in Parrotlets

Signs of ill health in birds fall into several broad categories, and one should look for any changes in the following areas:

Overall appearance and / or posture:

- Sitting low on a perch
- Feathers are permanently ruffled
- Huddling
- Drooping wings
- Frequently or constantly elevated wings
- Sitting on the bottom of the cage rather than a perch
- Trembling or shaking
- Lumps
- Swellings
- Tucking the head under a wing while standing on both feet
- Hanging from the side of the cage by its beak rather than perching
- Dull and / or sunken eyes
- Change of eye colour
- Change in droppings (frequency, appearance, and odour)
- Some sort of protrusion from the vent (the opening for a bird's urinary, intestinal and reproductive tracts).

Behaviour and / or attitude:

- Weakness
- Inactivity
- Keeping its eyes closed even when awake
- Changes in or cessation of vocalisations
- Walking in circles
- Loss of balance: falling over when walking or off a perch
- Unsteady when perching, walking, or standing

- Not preening or bathing
- Obsessive picking at feathers and / or skin
- Not flying
- Seizures
- Collapsing
- Becoming more aggressive or submissive
- No or poor response to stimuli
- Increased sleeping.

Eating and drinking behaviour:

- Increased or decreased appetite
- Inability or difficulty in picking up and manipulating food
- Weight loss
- Drinking more, or less, than usual
- Diarrhoea or constipation
- Swelling or distention in the crop area (a pouch in the oesophagus or gullet that is part of the digestive system)
- Vomiting
- Regurgitation that is not for the purposes of feeding chicks
- Straining to defecate
- Discharge from the mouth
- The keel (breast bone) becomes prominent.

Droppings and urine:

The droppings that birds produce consist of three components. The first is urates, which are normally white or cream. Second, the urine is a liquid and clear. Finally, the faeces, which is thicker than the urates and in Parrotlets is normally dark green or brown depending on their diet.

- Change in colour of the urates, faeces, or urine
- Change in consistency. If droppings become very watery it is usually a sign of increased urination, not necessarily diarrhoea, which is indicated by much looser faecal matter. Hard faeces indicate that the bird is suffering from constipation.
- Undigested food in the droppings
- Blood in the droppings
- Droppings are smaller
- Increased urination

- Change in frequency: either more or fewer droppings.

However, keep in mind that there will be some natural variation in droppings in healthy birds that have a varied, nutritious diet. More on that later…

Breathing changes:

- Sneezing
- Discharge or build-up around the nares (nostrils)
- Wheezing
- Produces a clicking sound when breathing
- Difficulty breathing, especially after activity
- Breathing through an open beak rather than the nares
- Tail bobs when the bird inhales
- Its voice sounds different.

Feathers:

- Loss of feathers that is not part of a normal moult and result in bald patches
- Dull or abnormally coloured feathers
- Constantly fluffed or ruffled feathers
- Misshapen or broken feathers
- Cessation of preening
- Excessive feather picking
- Wet or matted feathers.

Changes in the head:

- One side of the head is not the same shape or size as the other side
- The bird flicks or twitches its head frequently
- Discharge from the eyes
- Squinting
- Keeping the eyes closed or half closed
- Loss of feathers or redness of the tissue around the eyes
- Beak looks flaky
- Beak becomes discoloured.

Legs and feet:

- Thickening of the skin
- Swelling
- Redness or rawness
- Sores
- Bleeding
- Flaking
- Discolouration
- Abnormal nail growth
- Lameness
- Hobbling or favouring a leg
- Frequently shifting from one foot to the other.

In addition to the above, one needs to be on the lookout for signs of injury such as bleeding, burns, or wounds from pecking or bites.

If symptoms persist and / or worsen, or you are in doubt about what the problem is, it's better to err on the side of caution and consult your vet.

Evaluating your Parrotlet's droppings

It does sound both bizarre and unappealing that you need to monitor and evaluate your bird's droppings each day. However, it is essential. The reason is that they can tell you so much about the health – or lack of it – of your pet.

Normal droppings

If your pet eats specially formulated pellets it will produce brown faeces that are soft in consistency. A diet that contains a high proportion of seeds will generate dark green faeces.

As indicated, the urine within the dropping is normally a clear liquid. If you feed your feathered friend vegetables and fruit the urine will remain clear but there will be an increase in the amount.

The urates, a waste product generated by the kidneys along with urine, should always be cream or white regardless of diet.

Abnormal droppings

You need to know what your Parrotlet's droppings normally look like before you can know when things are not as they should be. On the other hand, you don't want to become concerned unnecessarily either.

One also needs to use common sense. If a bird has just had a treat or meal of food that has a marked colour (such as berries) that may well change the colour of the droppings for a short time. Similarly, the droppings of babies being hand reared on a formula will be affected by their diet. The first droppings of the day can look atypical too.

The signs and changes in droppings that should not be ignored as they are an indication of a serious illness or condition are: blood in the droppings, changes in urine from clear to yellow or green, marked changes in frequency of droppings, more urine than urates or faecal matter in the droppings,

Common diseases and ailments

There are several illnesses and conditions that captive birds are prone to. Unfortunately, Parrotlets, although hardy, are not immune. Birds that are not properly fed or housed or that are stressed are more at risk as their immune and other systems will not be robust.

a) Dirty Face Syndrome

Symptoms

As the name would suggest, the symptoms of this syndrome are facial feathers that are broken, dirty, or missing. This applies particularly to the areas around the beak and eyes.

Causes

The most common cause of this problem is that the bird can't reach its food or water with ease. As a result, the bird pushes its face between the cage and / or substrate bars to try and reach its food and water or dropped food. At the very least this behaviour results in damage to the feathers.

The second possible cause is an underlying illness that is causing vomiting, regurgitation, or a runny beak or eyes.

Diagnosis

As the owner it should be easy to determine whether the position of the food and water bowl is the problem and, if so, put them somewhere else.

If they are not the issue, then you need to take your Parrotlet to the vet for a physical examination and any tests that may be required to make a firm diagnosis.

Treatment

Treatment will depend on what the underlying cause of the dirty face syndrome is.

Prevention

The best option is of course prevention rather than cure. Make sure that bowls are always easily accessible and take all the steps you can to safeguard your little bird's health.

b) Bumblefoot Disease

While this might sound like a slightly comical ailment, it is in fact a serious condition that affects the feet and nails. It is far more common in captive birds than in wild ones.

Causes

The tragic truth is that birds suffer from this potentially serious condition *usually* because they are not adequately or correctly fed or housed. The bad news is this diagnosis means the owner is not meeting his or her responsibilities. The good news is that it is in an owner's power to prevent the condition.

A possible cause is unsuitable perches that are too abrasive or even toxic. Certain woods are not suitable or free of chemicals and sandpaper perches are not a good option with these tiny birds. Perches that are too large in diameter for little feet can also cause damage.

One reason an all seed diet is not advised is that seeds are low in vitamin A, which keeps cells healthy. While vitamin A promotes health in the cells lining the respiratory, gastrointestinal, and urogenital tracts, it is also crucial for the health of epithelial cells, which form the top layer of the skin.

Vitamin A deficiency is one of the causes of bumblefoot. If the skin on the feet and legs is not strong and healthy it allows infections to enter the tissue. Depending on the nature and severity of the infection it can make a bird very ill or even kill it.

In addition to this vitamin, too much protein in its diet can also cause a bird to develop this condition. If there is too much stored protein in the body it leads to bacterial growth. These bacteria are then excreted through the skin. While feathers can absorb this, areas such as the legs and feet can't. Sores form under the feet and the tips and tops of the toes.

The other potential causes are very high levels of uric acid or a metabolic disorder of some kind.

Symptoms

Behavioural symptoms are an unwillingness or inability to stand or grip a perch with the affected foot or feet because of the pain caused by the condition.

The earliest visible physical symptoms are small pink or shiny patches on the bottom or top of the feet. There may also be a degree of swelling of the joints, toes, or the entire foot.

These abrasions can develop into open sores if left untreated. If these are exposed to bacteria, they will become infected. In a cage environment the most common bacterium is *Staphylococcus*. Once infected, the sores become inflamed and red and – in severe cases – blue or even black.

This type of advanced infection will result in permanent damage and distortion of the toes and feet. In the worst cases, the infection will erode the bone and cause systemic infections throughout the body, which is often fatal.

Treatment

Because of the potential for permanent damage and serious infection this condition must be treated by a vet as early as possible.

The most common treatment is antibiotics to deal with the infection. You may also have to make changes if there are perches that are too rough and the cage must be thoroughly disinfected. A vet will also ask about the patient's diet and may suggest changes if a deficiency is likely to be the cause of the condition. It may be necessary to perform surgery if the toes or feet have become very distorted.

Prevention

Preventative measures include selecting appropriate perches and keeping them clean, ensuring that your Parrotlet has a healthy and balanced diet, keeping the cage clean, and monitoring any changes in your pet's behaviour and the appearance of its toes and feet.

c) *Avian Gastric Yeast (AGY)*

This illness was known as Megabacteria because for many years it was thought to be caused by an atypical, large bacterium. It's now called Avian Gastric Yeast – AGY for short – or, to give it the full scientific name, as *Macrorhabdus ornithogaster*.

Causes

This serious, chronic, and potentially fatal disease is not caused by bacteria as was initially thought but by a type of yeast. It affects several species of birds that are popular pets, and Parrotlets become very ill very fast. This organism is mainly found in the narrow section between the two parts of the bird's stomach.

Symptoms

Although this is a condition that affects the gastric and digestive system, and causes ongoing weight loss, most birds with AGY appear to be eating well. The problem is that the food is not being digested correctly and therefore the bird is not getting any benefit from it.

With very small birds such as Parrotlets, weight loss can be hard to detect. However, the bird's droppings will also be affected, and this is easier for an owner and vet to detect. The faeces will often contain undigested food and sick birds may also develop diarrhoea or melena (a black tarry dropping).

Melena is the result of bleeding in the gastrointestinal tract caused by AGY. The condition and blood loss can also result in anaemia, which further weakens the bird. Very sick birds may also regurgitate food, blood, or mucous. General symptoms include weakness, ruffled feathers, lethargy, and head bobbing.

When the condition is very acute or severe the bird can be killed by it in a matter of one or two days. It is not understood why some birds become much sicker, much faster than others.

Diagnosis

A faecal examination, or several, is essential to accurately diagnose this condition. There are several tests available that detect this yeast in droppings. Some can be done during the examination.

Firstly, the vet can examine a fresh sample, mixed with saline solution, under the microscope and look for the presence of this yeast.

Secondly, a faecal cytology test provides a rapid result. On the downside, while this test method does identify very heavy infections, it may not detect light ones. The diagnosis might therefore not be made which would allow the condition to worsen.

Finally, a vet could use a Gram stain on a sample. This would identify both AGY and gastrointestinal bacteria. The drawbacks with this test are the same as those with the faecal cytology test.

The most accurate test is not one a vet can perform in his / her rooms. A Polymerase Chain Reaction or PCR test is a very sensitive and sophisticated test. It is most often used when a vet believes that AGY is the diagnosis but was unable to confirm it with the three tests described.

While this test is very accurate it does take several days to get the result, which is more time than very sick birds may have.

Treatment

Once a definite diagnosis has been made, treatment consists of an anti-fungal medication such as Amphotericin B. A course of treatment usually runs for 30 days. Fluconazole, also an anti-fungal, is sometimes used for birds that have not responded well to Amphotericin B.

A PCR test might be done at the end of a course of treatment to ensure that the infection has cleared completely.

If the illness is diagnosed correctly and early, the bird was previously healthy, and the infection is mild or moderate, the chances of recovery are good. Conversely, for birds that were not diagnosed or misdiagnosed and are very sick the prognosis may be poor.

Prevention

There is no vaccine that protects birds against this yeast infection. There are things you can do to protect your Parrotlet from AGY, or at least reduce the risk, but prevention is far from easy.

If you have bought a pet bird from a breeder, make sure that he or she is reputable and takes steps to protect his or her stock from illness. You need to know you have used a breeder that monitors the bird's health, has tests done, and takes immediate action to control and eradicate illness.

When you select a bird, take the time to watch it carefully for any signs of illness. If the breeder is prepared to do so, ask for tests to be done to look for AGY or ask to take the bird to a vet for a test. When you take your new bird home you must keep it away from your other birds for a month to prevent infection or cross-infection.

d) Psittacosis (Parrot Fever)

In addition to psittacosis, this disease is known as avian chlamydiosis and Parrot Fever. It's a serious illness and is found in birds and some mammals, including people.

Not only can this disease be contracted by different species it is also very easily spread. It can spread in several ways, including as particles in the air.

Causes

While other bacteria may cause this disease, the common culprits are three forms of *Chlamydophila*: *C. psittaci* (the most common one), *C. avium*, and *C. gallinacean*. Transmission is from bird to bird or bird to mammal.

Although it is the most common source of infection, a bird doesn't even have to come into direct contact with a sick bird to become infected. The illness can be spread to a bird or mammal if it is in contact with an item a sick bird has been in contact with such as feathers, droppings, water bowls, perches, and so forth. Most worrying is that the bacteria are also carried on airborne particles.

Symptoms

This illness can remain dormant for some time and the bird will not show any symptoms during this period. It is not uncommon that the symptoms will first appear when they bird is stressed.

Visible signs include lethargy, fluffed feathers, diarrhoea, a marked loss of appetite, swollen or puffy eyes, and nasal discharge. Some sick birds may also experience breathing problems. An examination usually reveals significant weight loss and an enlarged liver.

Diagnosis

Given the symptoms of psittacosis are the same as those for several other illnesses, a firm diagnosis can only be made by a vet after he or she has performed a physical examination and a range of tests. Tissue tests must be performed to detect the bacterium involved and to measure antigen and nucleic acid levels.

Some vets use a range of blood tests in addition to tissue and fluid cultures as a single test may not be conclusive or provide a definite diagnosis. In addition to blood, tests can be performed on droppings, excretions from the eyes, nose, urogenital tract, and tissue samples from various organs including the kidneys, lungs, liver, and spleen.

Treatment

If left untreated this illness is fatal in half the cases. However, once diagnosed it can be successfully treated with antibiotics. The choice of antibiotic will depend on which *Chlamydophila,* or other bacteria, has caused the infection.

A course of treatment usually lasts a long time. It is essential that the medication is given to the bird for the length of time specified by the vet or the infection may re-emerge.

Prevention

One's best defence against any kind of bacterial infection is good routine hygiene practices which include regular disinfecting of the cage, perches, bowls, etcetera. It's also crucial that you wash your hands before and after handling your Parrotlet and any other bird to prevent cross-infection.

Keeping your bird in a well-ventilated area will also minimise the chances of air borne contaminants circulating and infecting other birds or the mammals in your home (including you).

Quarantining a new bird for 30 days is also essential before you place it with other birds just in case the new arrival is a carrier but still asymptomatic. If one of your birds is diagnosed with parrot fever you must isolate it from the others to contain the disease.

e) Proventricular Dilatation Disease

Proventricular Dilatation Disease (PDD) is also known as Neuropathic Gastric Dilation and Macaw Wasting Disease as this species is particularly prone to the illness. This life-threatening condition attacks both the digestive tract and the central nervous system although sick birds may only show symptoms for one of the systems.

The proventricular is the glandular stomach in birds. It is connected to the oesophagus and produces gastric or digestive juices. PDD attacks the nerves serving the proventricular and other parts of the digestive tract. As a result, the muscles don't function properly. This in turn means that the sick bird can't digest and absorb food and nutrients normally.

Causes

This highly contagious illness is caused by the avian *Bornavirus*.

Symptoms

The symptoms of PDD are the result of both the virus itself and the bird's immune system's reaction to it.

General symptoms include lethargy and not responding to stimuli as usual. The inability to digest normally results in ongoing and severe weight loss. The gastric related signs include indigested food in the droppings and regurgitating food. Neurological symptoms include head tremors, ataxia (uncoordinated movements), an inability to perch or stand, seizures, and even paralysis.

Diagnosis

The vet will run several tests. X-rays may show an extremely enlarged or abnormal proventricular. Blood tests are used to identify the presence of the virus. A complicating factor is that some birds have avian *Bornavirus* in their body but aren't suffering from PDD.

Treatment

Treatment involves a combination of a special diet, anti-inflammatory medication, and antibiotics for any secondary infections. Sick birds must be kept in a stress-free environment and away from other birds to prevent the virus spreading.

Many birds with the disease will not survive and a vet may suggest euthanasia for birds that are very ill and suffering.

f) Broken blood feather

Pin feathers are also known as blood feathers. These are new feathers that are still growing and, as a result, have blood flowing into the shaft. Blood / pin feathers are especially common in young birds and during a moult.

While a broken feather ordinarily is not an emergency, it is if it's a blood feather. If the feather remains in the skin the hollow shaft allows a great deal of blood to flow out. Given birds are unable to cope with much blood loss, a bird can bleed to death if a broken pin feather is not dealt with very quickly.

Symptoms

The indication of this problem is blood on the bird or in its cage. In many cases the flow of blood from the broken feather shaft will be visible. If you see blood but can't find a blood feather, take your bird to the vet immediately.

Treatment

You must remove the feather shaft so that it no longer allows blood to flow freely. Wrap your bird gently in a suitable cloth so that you can keep him or her still.

When you are holding your feathered pet firmly you need to find the broken blood feather. Once you have identified the feather, grasp it firmly at the base of the shaft with tweezers or needle-nose pliers. Be careful not to grab hold of the skin. Pull the feather out as quickly as possible.

Place a pinch of corn starch on the area you removed the feather as this promotes blood clotting. Use clean gauze to apply gentle pressure to the area until the bleeding has stopped.

It's advisable to go to the vet afterwards to ensure there are no complications and that your Parrotlet is on the mend.

g) Polyomavirus

The parrot family are highly susceptible to *Polyomavirus* and baby and juvenile birds are particularly at risk. This fatal virus attacks multiple systems and organs at the same time. It also lowers the sick bird's immune system, which makes it vulnerable to bacteria, other viruses, parasites, and fungal infections. It is thought that it takes ten days to two weeks from exposure to developing symptoms.

Symptoms

The range of possible symptoms of *Polyomavirus* include loss of appetite, listlessness, tremors, paralysis, breathing difficulty, bleeding under the skin, abnormal feathers, regurgitation, weight loss, diarrhoea, excessive urination, dehydration, vomiting, and a swollen abdomen.

Death usually follows within a few days of symptoms emerging.

Causes

This virus is caught from infected birds or from their feathers, droppings, cages, nest boxes, and other contaminated items. This virus is also air borne and transmitted through particles from the feathers, skin, and cages of infected birds. An infected bird will also pass it onto her babies.

Treatment

This is a fatal condition and there's no treatment for it. Euthanasia is the kind and loving choice for a bird suffering from this condition.

Prevention

At time of writing a vaccine to protect against the virus is available. However, its effectiveness has yet to be proven. It's advisable to ask your vet about the possibility of a vaccine.

As with most illnesses the key to prevention is regular and rigorous cage hygiene. You need to disinfect the cage, perches, food and water bowls and so forth. While this virus is resistant to many disinfectants, chlorine bleach does work.

It's also essential to quarantine new birds and observe them for any symptoms of this dreadful disease.

h) Psittacine Beak and Feather Disease

Psittacine Beak and Feather Disease or PBFD is a highly contagious viral illness, which affects several species of birds but especially parrots.

The virus affects the feathers, beak, and immune system. It is usually young birds that become sick and, for reasons not yet know, birds over the age of three seldom become infected. Most birds that are infected die.

Symptoms

There are two forms of the disease and they have different sets of symptoms.

- *Peracute / acute form*: This is most likely to be found in juvenile parrots, and the symptoms have nothing to do with the feathers or the beak.

  In the peracute stage these little Parrotlets suffer from general depression, regurgitation, diarrhoea, and pneumonia.

  In the acute stage these young birds don't replace their down with healthy feathers. The new, emerging ones have lesions, are very painful and often loose, they break easily, and may bleed.

- *Chronic form*: Older birds are affected by this form of the illness. The powder-down feathers (the feathers closest to the body and underneath the other feathers) are often the first to be affected. They become broken easily, may bleed, and become deformed, curled, and discoloured. The feather follicles are damaged, and the sick bird becomes unable to replace them.

  In this form the beak is also affected. It may fracture, become elongated, or develop sunken areas. Parts of the interior beak tissue may die, forming brown patches. Given the beak tissue is so weakened other infections may occur in the beak and mouth.

In extreme cases, the nails on the feet can also be affected by the virus. There may also be a change in the colour and consistency of droppings as they can become green and contain mucous. Liver failure is not uncommon.

These birds may live for months or even years but become increasingly unwell, weak, and bald. Most die from secondary infections rather than from the virus itself.

Vets and owners may opt to end a bird's suffering rather than letting the illness run its course.

Causes

PBFD is the result of infection with the *Circovirus,* which is a DNA virus and one of the smallest disease-causing viruses. It attacks the immune system and the cells that produce feathers and make up the beak.

It is spread through both direct (birds in the same cage or the vicinity) and indirect (feather dust, droppings, etc.) contact with infected birds. Sick mothers may also pass it onto their babies.

Diagnosis

A medical history will be taken, and a thorough physical examination carried out. Conditions that have similar symptoms are ruled out as part of the diagnostic process. For example, some nutritional deficiencies, hormonal imbalances, and polyomavirus share symptoms with PBFD.

A blood count, a polymerase chain reaction or PCR test, and histopathology (an examination of tissue samples under a microscope) will reveal the presence of the virus or the type of cellular abnormalities it causes.

It should be noted that these tests are not infallible as there can be both false positives and false negatives due to factors such as air-borne contaminants. Your vet may opt to repeat them for confirmation.

Treatment

There is no treatment for PBFD. All medical care and dietary and environmental changes are geared to keep the bird as comfortable as possible and deal with inevitable secondary infections.

The disease is incurable and progressive and, as a result, euthanasia is often the best and kindest option.

Prevention

Ensure that you only purchase a Parrotlet from a breeder that screens his or her birds regularly for this virus. When you bring your new bird home, keep it in quarantine for 30 days to check for signs of ill health.

This nasty virus can't be eliminated with disinfectants and is difficult to control. It can also live outside a bird's body for years and spreads very easily.

A killed vaccine may be available in your area that can be administered to young birds. Ask your vet about the possibility of a vaccine.

i) Bird Parasites

Most living creatures can become infested with parasites and birds are no exception. There is a wide range of parasites, but the most common ones found in captive birds are:

- *Giardia*: This is a gastrointestinal parasite that is picked up by eating contaminated food and is very common in parrots. It is also a zoonotic organism meaning is can be passed on to humans.

  In both infested birds and humans, the symptoms are severe diarrhoea, dehydration, and weight loss. Bird's may also scratch more, pluck out feathers, and be more vocal than usual; all of these are signs of distress and discomfort.

  The best ways to prevent contamination are, firstly, by keeping your Parrotlet's cage and food and water bowls clean and, secondly, by protecting yourself by wearing gloves when cleaning and by washing your hands very thoroughly after handling your pet.

-   *Aspergillosis*: This parasite is a fungus called *Aspergillus* or Asper. It affects the respiratory system and is a common infection in captive parrots. The fungus grows in decaying plant and other matter and the spores are inhaled.

    The symptoms are flu-like: nasal discharge, crust and discharge around the eyes, difficulty breathing, weight loss, and abnormal droppings or diarrhoea.

    Vets use antibiotics to treat this infection and, if caught early, a bird will recover. However, an advanced or chronic case of Asper does not have a good prognosis.

    Prevention is based on good hygiene practices. One of the places this fungus will thrive is in the substrate of a cage that is not cleaned daily. You also need to wash all vegetables and fruits you feed your Parrotlet. Finally, wash your hands before and after cleaning the cage or any item from it and your feathery pet.

-   *Sarcocystis*: This parasite is less common in parrots but is the worst one as it can cause an infection that is fatal. What complicates diagnosis is that there are three different varieties. The first attacks the respiratory and pulmonary (lungs and heart) systems. The second affects the neurological (brain and nerves) system. The third invades the muscles.

    The symptoms will vary depending on which variety the bird is suffering from. The signs include breathing problems, poor mobility, yellow droppings, and lethargy. Death can occur very suddenly.

    As with Giardia, this parasite is zoonotic, so people can catch it from birds and vice versa.

General parasite prevention

These are very important and helpful and therefore bear repeating:

✓ Clean the cage and the water and food bowls daily

✓ Provide a nutritious diet so your bird is healthy generally and has a strong immune system

✓ Wash your hands before and after working with the cage and spending time with your Parrotlet.

j) Candidiasis

Candida is a yeast infection that primarily causes problems in the digestive tract but can also affect the beak and the respiratory system. Parrots, including Parrotlets, are unlikely to have eye, reproductive, skin, or feather issues the way other species do when they contract candida.

This condition is also more common in young birds, those with weak immune systems, and birds on an all-seed diet. Other risk factors are stress, a vitamin A deficiency, and / or poor cage hygiene.

Causes

The yeast responsible is *Candida albicans,* which is always present in the digestive system of birds. Low levels of this yeast are normal and healthy. If the level becomes too high the yeast causes damage to the digestive tract.

Symptoms

This infection may only affect one section of the digestive system or all of it.

If the beak and mouth are affected an infection may develop where the upper and lower beak join. The bird may also develop bad breath and raised, white patches inside the mouth. There may also be what looks like thick saliva or a whitish substance in the bird's mouth.

The signs of candidiasis in the lower digestive tract include diarrhoea, vomiting, loss of appetite, weight loss, depression, and – in chronic cases – malnutrition.

If the crop is infected the area may become distended and thickened, it will take a long time to empty or won't empty at all, the bird will lose its appetite, become depressed, and may regurgitate food.

Diagnosis

Finding *Candida albicans* in the digestive tract is not enough for a diagnosis. A vet will take tissue and fluid samples using swabs for culture. A microscope will be used to assess the levels of the yeast in the samples. Only a large reading will be considered a positive result. These tests will be used in conjunction with the standard medical history and physical examination.

Treatment

The primary treatment is antifungal medication. The vet will also offer guidance to reduce or eliminate risk factors. This might, for instance, include revising the bird's diet.

Prevention

By keeping the cage clean, protecting the bird from stress, and providing a balanced, nutritious diet you will significantly reduce the chances of your pet developing candidiasis.

k) Food anxiety

This is a behavioural problem that can lead to physical issues.

Causes

This condition is found in poorly or unsocialised birds, ones that are by nature very nervous or anxious, or individuals weaned too young.

Symptoms

If your Parrotlet has already eaten and / or still has food but still begs and calls for food, it's a pretty good sign that it is suffering from food anxiety.

Treatment

A technique called regression weaning may be necessary to deal with what is essentially an emotional problem. What is sometimes the most effective remedy – although it won't work with all birds – is to hand feed the individual exhibiting this behaviour. In other words, you will treat the bird as though it is a baby that needs to be hand fed before being fully weaned.

Doing this provides an opportunity to bond with the bird, reduce its anxiety, and reassure the owner that their pet is eating and getting a nutritious diet.

If you are concerned you could consult a vet, breeder, bird club, or an avian association about a course of action. If the vet is concerned about nutrition, he or she may recommend some sort of supplement.

l) Malnutrition

Malnutrition is, shockingly, the leading cause of death in captive birds. It should be remembered that 24 hours in your life is the equivalent of a week for your Parrotlet.

Not eating, or not getting the right foods, for this length of time can be life threatening and certainly has implications for a bird's general state of health.

Causes

Malnutrition is caused by not eating the correct foods, not eating enough food, or a combination of the two. Incorrect or inadequate nutrition results in illnesses that can affect one or more systems and organs. These include the skin, feathers, the digestive tract, the respiratory system, and the urogenital tract.

A bird may not be eating because of an underlying medical problem. However, it can be that their owner is not providing the care that the pet requires. One popular misconception amongst bird owners and people generally is that seeds provide all the nutrition a bird needs. Seeds are not a nutritious diet for birds because:

- *They don't contain vitamin A*: This vitamin is essential for keeping epithelial cells healthy. While one usually thinks of the skin in relation to this type of cell, they also line the urogenital, respiratory, and gastrointestinal tracts.

  If this layer of cells is weak or breaks down, the tissue they should protect – and the body as a whole – is vulnerable to infection and disease, which may be fatal.

- *They are very low in calcium:* Calcium performs several important functions.

  Firstly, calcium helps muscles to contract correctly. This is significant in terms of movement and mobility but also for the health and correct function of major muscles such as the heart.

  In addition, calcium is necessary to keep bones strong. A lack of calcium leads to osteoporosis, which makes fractures more likely.

  Finally, this mineral is essential when females are getting ready to lay as egg shell contains high amounts of calcium.

- *They are low in protein and high in fat:* Birds must eat a lot of seeds to get the protein that they need. Unfortunately, doing so results in them ingesting far too much fat.

  This causes weight gain, which places strain on the bird's joints and potentially on some organs. Even more serious, fat cells can work their way into organs and, in the worst scenario, this causes organ failure.

Symptoms

The signs of malnutrition depend on the severity of the condition and which cells and systems have been affected.

However, if an owner weighs their pet regularly they will notice weight loss, which is certainly an indication that something is wrong. Other symptoms may include lethargy, poor mobility, listlessness, sores, changes in droppings, breathing problems, and feather loss.

Treatment

The course of treatment will depend entirely on what cells or systems have been affected. The vet will determine treatment after a full examination. In extreme cases the bird can't be saved.

Prevention

Malnutrition is entirely preventable by providing a captive bird with a well-balanced, nutritious diet and feeding it regularly. This is one of the core responsibilities of any pet owner.

Seeds should be kept to a minimum (approximately 20 to 30% of food) and mixed into the other food very thoroughly. Seeds are the junk food of bird nutrition and they will eat them first – or only them if that is an option!

All birds, including Parrotlets, require a varied diet to meet their needs and make life interesting for them. As far as possible you need to recreate the diet your feathered friend would have had in the wild. A healthy diet is discussed in chapter 9.

Diet conversion

Moving or converting a bird to a new diet is not a quick process and it can be frustrating for both owner and pet. It's especially challenging if you are dealing with a seed 'addict', but all birds are creatures of habit.

There are two basic options for moving your pet to a healthy diet. Your vet may be able to offer other ideas or draw up a plan specifically suited to your bird. Regardless of the method or process you use you need to:

- Observe your pet to ensure that he or she is eating

- Monitor the bird's droppings. Although colour and consistency will change thanks to a change in diet the volume should remain unchanged.

- Weigh your pet daily using an accurate scale that measures in grams. If your bird loses more than 10% of its body weight during the conversion process, take it to a vet.

One option is to gradually wean the bird off seed or the unhealthy food it is used to. One does so by mixing the feed it has been having into the new diet. Start with a 50 / 50 mix and decrease the amount of seed / non-nutritious food by 10% each week until only the new diet is being offered. This process usually takes two months or about eight weeks at the end of which the change-over will be complete.

A second method requires more work on your part, but it can also be very effective. Some owners feel, however, that this method is risky as it can result in weight loss. The first step is to remove all the food from the cage. In the morning one provides only the new diet. If, after two hours, the bird has not eaten, one adds a small amount of the bird's usual diet. That mix should only be left in the cage for an hour before all food is removed again. The same routine should be followed in the evening. One continues to do this each day until the bird is eating the new food.

m) Beak growth problems

The beak or rostrum of a bird is a very important part of its anatomy as it is used to eat, groom, in self-defence, play, and feeding babies. A healthy, strong beak is smooth, evenly coloured, symmetrical, and closes properly as the top and lower parts of the beak are correctly aligned.

However, sometimes beaks do not grow correctly, and this can cause problems for the bird. There are three conditions that are, unfortunately, not all that uncommon.

i. *Mandibula prognathism*: This condition occurs when the tip of the upper beak (the prognathism) rests on or even inside the tip of the lower beak (the gnatotheca).

    Cause: It is not known what causes this misalignment but is thought to be a developmental abnormality. As such it may be affected by a range of factors, including incubation problems and incorrect hand-feeding techniques. These theories carry more weight because the condition is very rare in birds raised by their parents. Genetics may, however, play a role.

    Treatment: The course of treatment is determined by the severity of the condition and the bird's age. It can be easier to remedy in young birds when the beak is still a little malleable.

    With youngsters one can use a finger to place gentle pressure on the upper beak to move it out. This should be done several times a day. Older bird's beaks have already hardened, and the only option may be some sort of appliance that must be fitted by a vet.

Prevention: If you are hand feeding a young bird be very careful not to place pressure on the beak that will result in distortion or malformation. Other factors are hard or impossible to prevent.

ii. ***Scissors beak***: This condition affects the upper beak (or rhinotheca) and causes it to move sideways or laterally. Although this condition is more common in other members of the parrot family, it has been reported in Parrotlets.

Cause: As with mandibula prognathism, the causes are not clear but are most likely to be developmental (incorrect incubation or hand feeding) or genetic. Other possibilities are trauma / injury to the beak, infection, or calcium deficiency.

Treatment: Again, treatment will be dictated by severity and the age of the bird. Gentle pressure from a finger several times a day on a youngster's beak may correct the angle of the beak. Beaks that have already hardened will require surgery and the fitting of a corrective appliance by a vet.

Prevention: Care should be taken when incubating eggs and hand feeding babies. Ensuring the correct diet will also help to prevent this malformation.

iii. ***Overgrown beak***: While it is usually the upper beak that becomes overgrown, the lower beak can also be affected. This condition makes eating, grooming, etcetera hard for the bird.

Normally a bird's beak is kept to the correct length through normal activities such as eating, chewing, grooming, and even instinctively rubbing their beak on a hard surface.

Cause: There are several possible causes: trauma, infection, a developmental abnormality, poor diet, or some underlying medical problem.

Treatment: If there is an underlying medical issue, that must be addressed separately. The only remedy for a beak that has become overgrown is trimming it and removing any flaking material. Given beak tissue, like human fingernails, does not feel pain it is not a painful process for a bird if done correctly.

However, it is better to have your bird's beak trimmed by a vet or someone with experience because if a beak is trimmed too radically and made too short it will be painful, will bleed, and the bird won't be able to eat.

Prevention: Correct nutrition and routine beak care are the only ways to prevent beak overgrow if your bird's usual habits are not keeping its beak at the right length. Another helpful step to take is to provide chew toys, as they will help to maintain healthy beak length.

You also need to check his or her beak every day; look for signs of overgrowth, discolouration, cracks, or excessive flaking. If you think your pet's beak is becoming overgrown or growing asymmetrically consult a vet before your bird's ability to eat and groom is compromised.

n) Beak injury or trauma

It is not unusual for birds to hurt their beaks, and the nature and the severity of the injury can depend on how it happened.

Causes

Beaks can be damaged by flying into a hard surface, a fight with another bird or an animal, chewing something very hard or through an electric cord, or getting the beak stuck and injuring it trying to get free.

A beak may suffer a puncture wound, be fractured, or even torn fully or partly away. Injured or damaged beaks bleed – badly in the case of severe injury – and they usually require cauterisation to stop the bleeding. If you attempt to cauterise your bird's beak yourself don't use silver nitrate sticks, as silver nitrate is toxic to all birds.

Treatment

Beak trauma should be treated by an avian vet. He or she will stop the bleeding, clean the wound, apply an antifungal, and prescribe antibiotics if necessary.

Because the bird's beak will be very painful it will struggle to eat so you will have to monitor its intake and weight very carefully. In the case of a beak that has been badly damaged the vet will perform surgery and use acrylics to carry out repairs. Punctures and cracks will heal with time as healthy, new tissue replaces the acrylic.

In very severe cases where the beak has been ripped off entirely, euthanasia may be the best option.

Prevention

There are several steps you can take to minimise the chances of beak trauma:

- ✓ Keeping your bird's beak strong and healthy should mean that an injury will be less severe

- ✓ Take immediate action if your pet is being harmed by another bird or animal

- ✓ Mark or cover windows and other surfaces the Parrotlet could fly into

- ✓ Ensure the gaps between cage bars are correct so the bird's head can't get stuck.

o) Beak problems caused by underlying conditions

Problems with beak health and shape can be caused by other medical conditions. For instance, abnormal beak growth may be a result, or even a symptom, of malnutrition, liver disease, or even liver problems.

Your vet will need to carry out an examination and perform tests to establish the true cause.

p) Egg binding

Egg binding is a reproductive condition that causes the egg to remain in the reproductive tract. This means that the egg cannot be expelled in the usual way.

While this problem is more common in large parrots, it does sometimes happen with Parrotlets.

Symptoms

The usual symptoms are a distended or swollen abdomen and frequent tail dipping or wagging.

The signs may be different if the egg is pressing on a nerve. This might affect the bird's legs, causing weakness or even paralysis.

Cause

The cause of egg binding is not complicated: it is due to a calcium deficiency, which results in the hen being unable to expel the egg naturally.

Treatment

This is not a condition that can be treated at home. An attempt to remove an egg by someone who is not sufficiently skilled or knowledgeable may result in internal injuries, paralysis, or even death. You need to take your bird to a vet.

The vet will locate the egg and assess its size using x-rays. Non-invasive techniques will be used first to get the bird to expel the egg the natural way. The vet may give the bird calcium and fluids and place it in a warm and humid environment. Another or additional option is to give the bird female hormones.

If these steps don't work, or the egg is simply too large, the vet will extract the egg manually or surgically.

Prevention

It is essential to ensure that your Parrotlet always has access to sufficient calcium. Cuttlefish are a very good source, but you can also obtain mineral blocks from a good pet store or some vets.

q) Bird lice and mites

Bird lice and mites are both parasitic insects that feed on skin, blood, and feathers. Unlike other lice, bird lice have biting rather than sucking mouth parts. Luckily these tiny bugs don't carry other diseases the way fleas and ticks do.

Most bird mites only live for about three weeks without a bird to feed on, and – fortunately – don't use humans as hosts. However, a mite may give a person a test bite, which involves the injection of saliva. This often results in a very itchy bite, which can be accompanied by a rash.

Symptoms

There may be no signs at all that your pet has lice or mites. However, some owners report seeing these insects moving around in the bird's feathers. If the infestation is very severe the bird may injure itself, including feathers and skin, by excessive scratching.

Treatment

Consensus is that over the counter remedies are not effective; some may even be harmful. You will need to take your Parrotlet to the vet to be properly treated.

The difficulty is that unless you have taken other measures the problem may re-emerge very soon after your pet gets home. These little pests will be waiting in your bird's cage and in your home for a bird host. The only remedy is to clean every surface of the cage (including the corners, perches, and so on) and to call in a fumigator to rid the entire home of pests.

Prevention

The only way to reduce the likelihood of your bird picking up lice or mites is by keeping the cage scrupulously clean.

5) *Zoonotic diseases*

This is a group of diseases that can be caused by fungi, bacteria, viruses or parasites. What distinguishes them from other diseases is that they can be transmitted from animals to humans or humans to animals. In other words, they pose a risk to your Parrotlet, you, and your family.

You can protect yourself by following a few simple but essential practices and teaching children to do the same:

➢ Wear gloves when you clean the cage, food and water bowels, and any other items from the cage

➢ Wash your hands very thoroughly with soap and warm water after cleaning the cage, handling your bird's toys, and after petting your pet

➢ Always keep the cage clean

➢ Don't eat, drink, or smoke when cleaning the cage, handling objects from the cage, or your Parrotlet

➢ Ensure children wash their hands correctly.

If you follow all these steps, the chances of picking up an illness from your feathered friend are very low. There are, however, certain individuals and groups that are more at risk of infection. These include the elderly, babies and very young children, those with chronic illnesses, or those undergoing treatments such as chemotherapy or organ transplants who have poor immune systems or susceptibility to infection respectively.

The most common zoonotic conditions passed from bird to human or vice versa are:

Psittacosis or Chlamydiosis

This illness was discussed from the perspective of a sick Parrotlet. However, it's also necessary to do so from the point of a person infected with this illness.

Cause

This *Chlamydia* is called *Chlamydia psittaci* because it is almost exclusively found in the parrot or *psittaci* family of birds. It is not the same chlamydia organism that is sexually transmitted in humans.

The most common way people catch this nasty infection is by inhaling the bacteria that are released into the air from the droppings and shed feathers of sick birds. A human can't pass the disease to another person or infect a bird.

The incubation period is between a week and a month. During this period there are unlikely to be any symptoms.

Symptoms

Some people infected with this bacterium will only develop a mild form of the illness with no symptoms, while others will become very ill indeed with symptoms and complications developing.

Symptoms are flu-like and include: fever, headache, chills, a cough, fatigue and listlessness, muscle aches, and shortness of breath.

While it is a lung infection, complications of untreated psittacosis include inflammation of the brain (such as meningitis), heart, kidneys, or liver. These organs may even be damaged more permanently.

Diagnosis

This illness is not too difficult to diagnose through blood tests and x-rays of the chest / lungs.

Treatment

Fortunately, this bacterium responds readily to antibiotics. In those with a mild to moderate infection the symptoms should start to ease within 24 hours and clear completely very rapidly.

Prevention

At time of writing there is no vaccine against this disease. The best way to prevent contracting this illness is by handling a bird infected with the bacterium as little as possible. When you clean out the cage you must wear gloves (as usual) and, if possible, a mask that will stop you breathing in any contaminated dust.

Your sick Parrotlet must of course also be treated or you will keep on infecting each other. If you suspect your feathery pet has psittacosis or is a carrier you must take him or her to the vet.

Cleanliness and hygiene is also crucial. You will have to disinfect the cage (all surfaces), water and food bowls, perches, and accessories such as toys. Remember to wash your hands very thoroughly with soap and warm water after you have cleaned the cage or something from it or handled your unwell pet.

Finally, having the illness does not mean that you or your little parrot will develop antibodies; you can be re-infected and get the condition again.

Mycobacterium Avium Complex or Avian Tuberculosis

Mycobacterium Avium Complex (MAC) is a bacterium that is related to the one that causes tuberculosis (TB). The MAC bacteria are commonly found in water, soil, and food and all of us have some in our bodies. Normally they don't cause illness, but if an individual has a very poor or compromised immune system they can become seriously ill.

Cause

This infection is caused by *Mycobacteria*. In addition to being found normally as mentioned above, it is also spread by the droppings of infected birds and air borne particles from their cages.

Symptoms

Symptoms of this illness vary depending on which part of the body becomes infected. In most cases it affects the intestines, lungs, or even the bones. In rare cases the infection spreads throughout the body.

This widespread form of the illness may cause anaemia, swollen glands (especially under the jaw), fever, night sweats, chills, fatigue, abdominal pain, diarrhoea, and weight loss. Those who become very ill may also suffer from pneumonia, hepatitis, or blood infections.

Diagnosis

Because several other illnesses can have the same signs and symptoms as MAC a physical examination coupled with tests is necessary to make a firm diagnosis.

These tests may be performed on fluids (blood, urine, sputum) or tissue samples from the affected site or area. These tests involve bacterial cultures being carried out in a laboratory, sophisticated tests such as these take a few weeks.

More immediate tests may be performed including standard blood tests such as a blood count to rule out problems such as anaemia. X-rays and scans are also very useful diagnostic tools, as they will identify problems with internal organs such as the liver, lungs, spleen, and lymph nodes.

Treatment

Quite often a combination of two or three antibiotics is used to treat these bacteria.

In some cases when the patient has a very weak immune system, the treatment will be long term: an initial treatment to control the infection and the maintenance medication for up to a year. In those patients with HIV or AIDS the treatment will be for the rest of their lives.

Prevention

Because MAC bacteria are so common they can't be avoided. People with compromised immune systems should not be allowed into the room or area where an infected bird is kept.

What makes it problematic is that some birds that contract this illness show no or minimal symptoms. However, a vet may recommend that a bird that has been diagnosed with this condition be euthanised because of the risk it poses to humans and other birds.

Campylobacteriosis

Campylobacteriosis is a bacterial infection that is contracted when one eats food or drinks water that has been contaminated by the droppings of birds that carry the disease. It is more often a result of eating undercooked poultry such as chicken, but it can be caught from pet birds.

Those more at risk of becoming ill – or more seriously ill – are babies, young children, those with weak immune systems, and (strangely) men. It's also a more common health problem in the summer months.

Cause

Campylobacter is found in the digestive system of some birds, including poultry, and cattle.

If droppings or other faecal matter contaminates areas where food is prepared, drinking water, or items used to prepare or eat food, these bacteria are passed on.

Symptoms

While those with a mild case may not experience any symptoms, others infected with this bacterium will experience fever, bloating, stomach cramps, nausea, vomiting, diarrhoea, and – in severe cases – stools may become bloody.

If severe, ongoing symptoms are left untreated patients may become dehydrated or complications may develop. A doctor should be consulted if the fever is very high ($102°$ Fahrenheit or $39°$ Celsius), the abdominal pain is severe, or the diarrhoea and / or vomiting has lasted for more than two days.

Certain individuals who are more susceptible to infections may develop complications such as gall bladder problems.

Diagnosis

Because most of the symptoms could indicate other medical issues, tests are necessary to make a definitive diagnosis.

The most common one is that the doctor will request a stool sample which will be sent to a laboratory where a culture to identify the specific bacterium will be carried out.

Treatment

In most cases, no medication is necessary as the illness runs its course over a few days or maximum ten days.

It's important to guard against dehydration by drinking lots of fluids. Unless advised to do so by a doctor it is not a good idea to use medication to stop the vomiting or diarrhoea, as they are the body's natural way of getting rid of this type of infection.

Prevention

As with so much else the key to prevention is good hygiene practices.

Hand washing is crucial. Always wash your hands with soap and warm water, even if you wear gloves, after coming into contract with bird droppings. If anyone in your family has diarrhoea make sure that they are even more fastidious about hand washing than usual.

Secondly, don't ever wash bird's water or food bowls or any items from the cage where they could contaminate food utensils or preparation surfaces. This includes using sinks where people's dishes are washed.

Three less common infections worth mentioning...

Histoplasmosis

This illness also affects the respiratory system and is caused by inhaling the spores from the *Histoplasma* fungus that are released from contaminated soil, dust, nesting material, or bird droppings.

Fortunately, this condition is rare in captive birds and can be avoided by keeping cages free of any build-up of droppings and not placing a cage or aviary near where droppings and other debris left by wild birds, especially pigeons, accumulate.

Cryptococcus

Like Histoplasmosis, this condition is also caused by a fungus and is found more in wild birds and particularly in pigeons. These spores and 'fungal dust' are also present in, and released from, accumulated droppings.

Symptoms in pet birds include diarrhoea, tremors, seizures, and even paralysis. In humans the inhaled fungus causes lung and breathing problems and can even cause very serious brain conditions such as encephalitis and meningitis.

Allergic Alveolitus

This is not a true zoonotic illness in that birds don't develop the disease. People contract it from inhaling particles of bird dander (dust from feathers, skin cells, and so on).

The symptoms are like those of other allergies and can include itchy and / or red eyes, runny nose and / or eyes, sneezing, coughing, and nasal congestion. In severe cases breathing may be affected.

6) Dealing with a bite or scratch from your Parrotlet

It may seem odd to call it a bite when Parrotlets have no teeth, but a nip from a sharp, strong beak is a painful experience and it can cause damage. Their claws are also deceptively sharp.

In addition, birds often have bacteria in their mouths, on their beaks, or under their nails, which can infect a wound. The possibility of infection is more of a concern, usually, than the wound itself. In the event of a bite or a scratch that has broken the skin you need to:

- Immediately wash the wound very thoroughly with soap and water

- If the bird that bit or scratched you looks, or is, ill or if the wound bleeds profusely or is very deep you should see your doctor

- A wound site that becomes red, swollen, hot, or starts to ooze requires assessment and treatment by a medical professional as these are signs of infection

- It's also a good idea to see a doctor for a tetanus booster if it's more than 5 years since your last one.

If medical attention is needed it's important to tell the person treating you that the bite or scratch is from a bird.

7) Parrotlet First Aid

While one can't prepare for every eventuality, it is a good idea to know what to do and to keep a first aid kit handy so that you can treat your pet immediately if the need arises.

First Aid

In an emergency you may need to care for your bird until it can be seen by a vet. The most important needs for a sick or injured bird are warmth, minimal handling, quiet, and food.

85° to 90° Fahrenheit or 29° to 32° Celsius is considered the optimal temperature range for sick birds.

Unless you need to staunch bleeding or restrain an ill or hurt bird just let it sit quietly so that it is not stressed or hurt.

Food is also important. The difficulty is that a Parrotlet that won't eat is already very sick or has been badly injured. In this situation, offer your pet its favourite treats to tempt it to eat. With some birds you may need to resort to hand feeding. However, don't ever force a bird to eat or give it liquid food.

An Avian First Aid Kit

By taking the right action immediately your little parrot has a better chance of making a full recovery. While suggestions as to content will vary depending on who you ask, the following items appear on most lists:

- Styptic powder (to stop feather or toe nail bleeding)
- Medical scissors
- Antiseptic wipes
- Sterile gauze
- Cotton swabs
- Bandages in a variety of different sizes
- Tweezers
- Eyedropper
- Triple antibiotic ointment
- A small bag of food (ensure it's your pet's favourite treat and always fresh)
- Vet bandage wrap
- Small flashlight with an extra set of batteries
- Bottle of hydrogen peroxide
- Q-tips
- Magnifying glass

- A plucking instrument (tweezers, locking forceps, or needle-nose pliers)
- Hand sanitising wipes
- Latex gloves
- Eye and skin wash (to flush out wounds or eyes).

It's a good idea to ensure that any products, powders, or solutions you include are safe for use on birds. An avian vet or Parrotlet breeder will be able to help you with this.

When you have obtained all the items on the list above, you need to place them all into a suitable container. It's not necessary to get anything expensive or purpose-manufactured. The container must be clearly labelled, closed securely, and keep the contents dry and clean; that's all you need. All that remains is to keep the kit somewhere it is easy to access quickly.

A very helpful addition, although you could keep this somewhere else that is both safe and handy, is a list of all the important emergency and other contact numbers. In an emergency one is not always thinking clearly so having the numbers you need to hand can save precious time. Have a card or list that includes your vet's number (including an after-hours or emergency number), the pet poison helpline and any other local resources that would be useful.

Chapter 11: Reproduction & Breeding

Those fortunate enough to have Parrotlets and have both a male and a female that are a mating or a bonded pair may be tempted to breed them. On the other hand, you may not want to breed these feisty little parrots, but your mated pair do what comes naturally and you find yourself becoming an unintentional breeder!

Although this species of parrot reaches sexual maturity at around ten months that is too young to breed them. These birds should be at least a year old and Mexican and Yellow Faced birds do better if they don't breed until they are about two years old.

1) Reproduction

Not all types of Parrotlet have a specific breeding season. The Pacific Parrotlet breeds from January to May, but others will mate and lay eggs all year round except in the height of summer.

Birds will begin mating displays, which involve both specific mating behaviours or postures and, in the case of the male, changes to the colour of the plumage on the rump. Once birds are paired, the female will look for a suitable nest site.

Parrotlets do not build nests. Rather, they find hollows in trees or a suitable cavity in either a natural or man-made structure. Alternatively, a hen will select the abandoned nest of another bird. She will, however, clean the nest area carefully and enlarge it if necessary. The nest is not lined with materials such as grass, moss, etcetera the way other birds do.

The female will typically lay a batch of four to six eggs on the floor of the nest. Some hens may lay as many as nine eggs. She will remain alone in the nest for the incubation period of 17 to 24 days depending on the species. Her mate stands guard outside and brings her food during this period.

Once hatched, the babies are fed by both parents until they are old enough to leave the nest and feed. The young learn to feed by watching and copying their parents. This takes on average four to five weeks after the eggs hatch. By six to eight weeks the babies will be completely weaned.

In wild birds, a second clutch of eggs may be produced as soon as a week after the first brood has left the nest.

2) Breeding Parrotlets

If you made the decision to invest in one or more mated or bonded pairs specifically to breed these little birds, it's good to know that it's not too difficult. So long as the birds are healthy, and their nutrition and environment are right, they will produce young. Wild caught birds are fine for breeding even though they don't make good pets.

It is, however, essential to make sure that you have a "true pair". In other words, they must be the same species to prevent problems with offspring and to keep the species or sub-species pure. Hybrid bird species are unlikely to thrive.

The second option, if you bought young birds, is to pair or bond them together once they are sexually mature and old enough. It's not a good idea to breed with very young birds. This is especially true for hens, as immature birds may become egg bound.

Although they don't want to be crowded, bothered, or watched when breeding, these birds will be comfortable with breeding in a cage or aviary environment so long as they have the space and conditions that they require.

There are breeders that say that you shouldn't give breeding birds toys, while others state that these pets still need to be entertained to prevent boredom and frustration. It may depend on the individual bird or pair and their state of mind.

When they are about five weeks old the young will fledge. In other words, they have all their feathers and can leave the nest. The fledglings will teach themselves to feed by copying their parents. By eight weeks on average the young are weaned completely.

Young birds should not be taken from their parents before they are fully weaned. They need to receive the nutritional benefits of the mother's crop milk to build strong immune systems, bones, feathers, and organs.

Weaned young should be placed in a separate cage for a while and monitored closely to ensure that they have made the transition and are eating properly.

3) Sexing Parrotlets

Once the pin feathers begin to grow and open it is possible to sex the young and to determine what colour they will be as adults. After the first month of their lives they have all their juvenile plumage. Youngsters moult twice in the first year of their lives. After the second moult they have their full adult plumage and sex markings.

Thanks to the dimorphic nature of the Parrotlets the obvious sex markings in the plumage make sexing these little birds easy. There is no need to do genetic or surgical sexing although DNA testing is required with the Albino Pacific Parrotlet, as there is no colour in the plumage at all.

Except for this species all males have some degree of blue on their rumps and secondary blue sex markings on their wings. Yellow Faced Parrotlet females are the only hens that have blue wing markings. However, they are much paler than the male's.

4) Pairing & bonding

In terms of bonding, there is no evidence that these pint-sized parrots are monogamous. For this reason, there are breeders that keep the males and females in separate cages until breeding season. Some breeders have a more romantic view and believe that their mating pairs do bond for life. For this reason, the breeder keeps them together all year round. The best advice might be to be guided by the temperaments and behaviour of the birds in question.

With birds that are kept apart and then placed into breeding cages – especially if the birds have been kept with their own sex – the male should be placed in the cage first. The female can be placed in the cage a few days later. This should reduce or eliminate any territorial disputes between them and increase the chance of successful bonding.

A mating pair may form a strong bond and, in addition to raising the young together, they will spend time together and groom each other. Rather like people, even strongly bonded Parrotlet couples can be feisty and argumentative. These small scraps can be ignored.

While these colourful small birds may be sociable flock birds ordinarily, this is not the case when they are breeding. Mexican Parrotlets are the exception but other than them, males can become very aggressive when they are protecting the hen, nest, and eggs or babies. As a result, each breeding pair *must* have their own cage and not be able to see into the other cages.

5) Breeding cages

While these colourful small birds may be sociable flock birds ordinarily, this is not the case when they are breeding. Mexican Parrotlets are the exception but other than them, males can become very aggressive when they are protecting the hen, nest, and eggs or babies. As a result, each breeding pair should have their own cage and not be able to see into the other cages.

The cage should be very similar in décor to the one the birds are used to. In other words, there should be branches / perches, water and food bowls, and toys. This will help to keep the pair relaxed and happy. Feeling stressed can interfere with the breeding process or even result in health problems.

The breeding cages need not be as large as the ordinary cages, but there must still be enough space for flight and normal activity. Cage cleanliness and hygiene of course remain essential.

6) Breeding cage placement

Because breeding pairs need to be stress free (and prefer a little privacy) it's preferable for pairs not to be able to see each other. This physical and visual separation also reduces aggressive and territorial behaviour between cages.

If birds can see neighbours, and they perceive them as a threat, more time and energy will be spent in fighting or territorial displays than in breeding.

In rare cases males have been known to kill their mates or babies in an outburst of extreme aggression when a male neighbour is perceived as a threat or rival.

If there isn't enough space to separate breeding cages, it is necessary to at least place a visual barrier between them. The divider that you use must be solid. Although it's not usually problematic if the birds can hear each other, they mustn't be able to see each other.

7) Nest or breeding boxes

Size and shape

In terms of size, consensus is that nesting boxes should be a minimum of 20 x 18 x 18 inches or 51 x 46 x 46 centimetres with an opening of 1 ½ to 2 ½ inches or 4 to 6 centimetres.

Some breeders use a horizontal nesting box and others favour using an L-shaped one. The box does need to be deep enough to keep the eggs safe and to make the hen feel secure.

Substrate or nesting material

In the wild the floor of the nest is bare. Nevertheless, there are breeders that place some sort of material in the nest box to cushion the eggs and prevent them from moving around. A popular choice is wood shavings.

In many cases the female will throw all or most of the nesting material out of the box before laying her eggs. You can replace the material with the same type, try a different substrate, or just leave her be if replacing the nesting material appears to be causing her or the male stress.

Using the nesting box

If you have a bonded pair that stay together in a cage all year, they may use the nest box to sleep in at night when they are not breeding. Very shy or anxious birds may use the nest box to hide in. Yet other couples won't go into the next box at all until it is time to breed and lay.

In some case the male will go into the nest box first to inspect it. With other birds the female will enter first to 'prepare' the nest. Other females will enter the nest box and stay there; eggs often follow soon thereafter.

There are also pairs that will mate in the privacy of the nest box. To safeguard their privacy – or sense of it – place the nest box where the opening of the box is not facing an adjoining cage or near an area of activity or traffic.

Nesting box hygiene

It's important to keep the nest box clean, but it's equally – perhaps more – important not to disturb or stress the female while she is laying and incubating eggs. The male, who is guarding her and the eggs, may also become aggressive and stressed because of the intrusion.

That said, you need to carry out routine hygiene while respecting the physical and emotional state of breeding birds. A clean nest box is essential for the health of the female and the hatchlings. Any nesting material that has become dirty, droppings, and old food must be removed to prevent health and contamination issues.

A nesting box must be very thoroughly cleaned and disinfected after each clutch of eggs has hatched and the babies are fledged and / or after a female has laid unfertilised eggs that she has then abandoned.

Diluted bleach (80% water and 20% ordinary commercial bleach) is a good option to clean and disinfect both the exterior and interior of the box. It's not necessary to rinse the box, but it must be very thoroughly dried.

Cleaning the nesting box after hatching

It can be very nerve-wracking to clean the nest box after the eggs hatch. However, you need to remove all debris to keep the parents and babies healthy. Droppings and other debris builds up very fast in nest boxes as there are two adults and the hatchlings.

The secret is to remove the babies with great care and place them in a container lined with clean nesting material. The container should be the right size to prevent the babies falling or getting out. Leave the container in the cage so that the parents can see the babies so that, hopefully, they will not become as anxious or stressed.

Clean the nesting box out by removing all soiled nesting material and droppings. Don't use bleach or any other disinfectant products until the young are weaned, fledged, and out of the nesting box permanently.

8) The reproductive process

Mating season

As previously stated, there is no specific or defined breeding season for the various species of Parrotlets. This means that they can mate and lay eggs all year. Breeders, however, recommend that captive birds be limited to no more than three clutches a year.

Number of clutches per year

Breeding depletes the female's supply of minerals, nutrients, and fats. Therefore, producing eggs too frequently will affect her health negatively and could even reduce her life expectancy. In addition, giving the parents a chance to rest and build up their reserves between batches results in healthier, stronger babies.

Breeders also need breaks between batches as there is a great deal of work involved in monitoring a mating pair and, subsequently, caring for and feeding the babies. Some breeders opt to begin their breeding program in spring and end it mid or late summer.

Mating

Mating itself will usually take place in the nesting box. Often the male will go in first and then call, inviting the female to join him. Unlike with other species, including other birds, the male does not sit on the female's back during mating. Parrotlets are unique in that they mate sideways with the male alongside the female.

Signs that the hen is going to lay

A hen that is ready to lay eggs will appear 'fat', the vent area becomes swollen, and – often – the female's droppings increase dramatically in size.

Laying

Not all the eggs are laid at once although two eggs may be laid on the same day. Eggs are laid every other day until the clutch is finished, and the female will produce four to six eggs over several days.

This is the usual clutch size although clutches of ten eggs have been reported. The hen may not sit on her eggs until the second or even the third one has been laid.

There may be also be clutches of clear eggs which are not fertile. It's not unusual for a pair to produce several clutches of infertile eggs over a few breeding cycles before they have chicks.

Missing or broken eggs

If the parents are very young or inexperienced there is the possibility that the eggs may be broken or that the chicks could be harmed. The destruction of eggs may be accidental or deliberate.

A broken egg may be eaten by the hen. It is believed that she does this to keep the nest box clean. However, a bird that eats an egg is likely to do so again. This behaviour is extremely hard to stop and, as a result, these birds must be removed from the breeding program.

If the pair is deliberately destroying their eggs you may need to intervene. Some breeders replace newly laid eggs with rubber ones. Usually the parents learn that the eggs can't be broken, and they stop trying.

With some pairs the destructive behaviour stops of its own accord or does not recur with subsequent clutches. If only one parent is destroying the eggs it is necessary to remove him or her.

Incubation

This, like much else with breeding, varies from female to female. Some Parrotlet mothers will sit on the eggs from the beginning and the laying of the first egg. Others will be far slower to sit.

If the female does begin incubating her eggs immediately, and it is a large clutch, it can cause increased age differences between the first egg and the last one to be laid several days later.

Most species incubate eggs for an average of 18 days. Mexican Parrotlets incubate for longer at about 22 days. Regardless of species, the female won't leave the nest box during this time except to defecate.

The male feeds the female at the entrance of the nest box or even inside it. He may sleep inside the nest box with his mate and, in extremely rare cases, he may even share incubation duties.

Hatching

If the female begins incubating after the first two or three eggs are laid, these eggs may all hatch at the same time. While the female sits on the eggs the male stands guard.

Once all the eggs have hatched the babies will be fed by both parents. Both play a role, as described earlier, in producing the ideal mix of nutrients for the hatchlings.

Because the pair are working hard to care for and feed their brood it is essential that you make sure that they have the food they need. An extra treat in the form of a favourite such as the ever-popular millet is a very good idea for busy bird parents.

The youngsters will grow quickly but should not be removed from their parents for hand feeding for at least two weeks.

Multiple clutches

Due to a lack of a limited breeding season there is the possibility that some pairs will continue to produce eggs one clutch after another. Birds need to rest between them and if they don't have the sense to do so they must be encouraged to.

The first solution to try is to remove the nesting box from the pair's cage. If they simply move breeding and laying activities to another area of the cage you need to get 'tougher'. In these situations, the pair should be moved to a different cage. The change of environment is usually sufficient to break the breeding cycle.

When to stop Parrotlets breeding

Most breeders state that the number of clutches annually must be reduced for the wellbeing of the pair, especially the female. However, in addition to this there comes a time when birds are too old to continue to produce fertile eggs and healthy, strong offspring.

Most breeders will only breed with a bird until it is about six years old or even as young as four depending on the individual. The absolute outside would be eight years. After a certain age there is simply too great a health risk to both the female and the offspring.

There will also be an increasing large number of eggs that won't hatch.

Ringing / banding hatchlings

Many breeders ring babies so that they can keep accurate records and follow lineage or blood lines. This helps to ensure that related birds are never paired as this can cause genetic and other health problems in the offspring.

Babies can be ringed when they are eight days old but other breeders suggest it should be done at 14 to 20 days. An M-size ring is usually used for Celestial / Pacific Parrotlets and L-size for Spectacled babies because the young of these species are slightly different in size.

You need to carefully put the three larger toes through the band, hold the small inside toe back against the foot, and slide the band over the foot and onto the ankle. Avian microchips are now available but are not in common use, especially for birds as small as Parrotlets.

You must use the correct size bands on youngsters because they are growing; you don't want the band causing constriction. It's also essential to ensure that the leg underneath the band is clean and the skin is healthy. Any signs of swelling, inflammation, and / or sores under, above, or below the band must be dealt with by a vet immediately.

It is important to note that if you have banded the chicks but its parents don't wear bands, you can't return the babies to the nest. The parents won't know what the band is and, in their frantic effort to get the strange object off their chick's leg the baby may get badly injured or even killed.

Parent raised chicks

There are breeders that chose to let the parent birds raise the babies themselves or at least the youngest of the clutch. There are both pros and cons to this.

On the upside this is a more natural way for the young to grow up. They will fledge but continue to sleep in the nest box with one or both parents. They will also be fed by the parent birds until they are weaned and feed on their own.

The potential problem – and it can be a serious one – is that the parents may harm or even kill the young. The father may become aggressive and violent towards male chicks, and the mother may try to drive the chicks out of the nesting box if she begins to lay another clutch. In either event you would have to step in and remove the young to protect them. You would then need to care for them.

Dealing with a broody hen

If you have a single, female bird her hormones are still going to affect her. She will get broody and lay eggs even in the absence of a male. A broody bird will look for a nesting site and may become shy and timid. There are things you can do to help her during these times.

Some owners remove the nesting box from the cage. Others take a less disruptive approach. Reducing the amount of light in the cage can reduce broodiness and laying cycles because the warmer months are more often breeding months. You could cover the cage earlier during these months, partially draw curtains or lower blinds, or use artificial light less in the room the cage is in. If your bird is going to lay she will need more sleep anyway.

Because eggs, whether fertile or not, draw nutrients and calories from the female's body, you need to ensure that she is eating well and getting enough calcium and vitamin D. If necessary, you can obtain a suitable supplement. Even if she is eating you must keep a close eye on her state of health and behaviour. Ensuring she has a good diet should guard against her becoming egg bound too.

Once the eggs have been laid, allow her to sit on them until she abandons them. She may incubate the eggs for a several days or even several weeks before losing interest in them. Once she has, remove the eggs. Don't remove the eggs from the nesting box while she is still incubating them. If you do, she will lay another clutch and the cycle will begin again.

Some owners replace the eggs with rubber or plastic ones. However, other people say they don't work.

9) Hand rearing babies

Hand reared and hand tamed are two entirely different things. Hand reared refers to taking the babies away from the parents and feeding them by hand. Hand taming refers to socialising birds so that they are 'tame' and bond with people.

It may seem counter-intuitive, but hand-reared Parrotlets don't necessarily make better pets. The reason is that it's an unnatural way of being raised and the babies may develop health and / or behavioural problems. It's also very hard work for the breeder.

Given hand rearing is a 24-hour commitment it should only be undertaken by the most dedicated and experienced Parrotlet breeders. This feeding regimen must continue until the young are fledged.

Chicks that are going to be hand-reared are removed from their parents when they are between 12 and 16 days old. It can be useful to leave the very youngest chicks (the ones that hatched last) with the parents to be reared by them.

Incubators: heating, humidity, types, and bedding

Temperature:

Because chicks are almost bald until their feathers grow in they need extra help with staying warm. If they get too cold they will get sick or die. The required temperature varies depending on age and environment:

- Newly hatched chicks: 35° to 36.5°Celsius or 96° to 98° Fahrenheit for several days
- Babies that are two to three days old: 33.5° to 35°Celsius or 92° to 96° Fahrenheit
- Youngsters under 2 weeks old: 32° to 33.5°Celsius or 90° to 92° Fahrenheit
- Nursery: 25.5° to 27.5°Celsius or 78° to 82° Fahrenheit.

Indications that a baby Parrotlet is overheated is that it will be restless or hyperactive and will pant. The skin may also look dry and red. Chicks that are too cold will shiver, won't ask for food, and will become very still or inactive. Cold results in digestive problems and sometimes death as it is very hard to warm up a baby that has got too cold.

Humidity:

Ambient humidity is also an important factor when caring for very new Parrotlets. In the wild or in nesting boxes with their parents and siblings, humidity levels are likely to be rather high. In captivity the heat provided for baby birds is often too dry.

Levels of 15 to 35% are too low, and humidity levels for hand reared babies should be in the 55 to 70% range. These higher levels result in much happier, healthier babies. They gain weight better, grow faster, and are quiet and content. Containers of water can be used in a nursery environment as sources of both humidity and warmth.

Incubators:

You can invest in a purpose-made incubator or make one yourself. There are a range of possibilities with both options. Incubators are available from specialist stores and the Internet offers ideas and diagrams for DIY versions. An incubator doesn't have to be specifically for birds as some breeders use ones designed for human babies. It will depend on your requirements and budget.

However, a word of caution about homemade incubators: don't use hot water bottles or heating pads to keep the chicks warm. Both can result in overheating (potentially fatal), burns, or even cold babies if the temperature is not frequently monitored. It is also much more difficult to measure and control humidity levels with the required accuracy.

In terms of size, smaller containers make disease control more achievable as they are easier to clean and to keep at the right temperature and humidity levels. You need a separate container for each clutch to prevent possible cross-infection.

Bedding

Chicks younger than 14 days can be placed on paper towels. These must be changed at each feeding so that the baby is not sitting in damp towel or faecal matter.

If paper towel does not allow the chick to stay upright or get a firm footing, you will need to reconsider the bedding type so that the chicks don't develop splayed legs or infections. Some breeders advocate using towels or wood shavings. Granular, nut shell, or corn bedding is not recommended at all as it can cause injuries. If the chick starts to eat the bedding it is often an indication that it is too hot or not getting enough and / or the right food.

Baby formula for chicks

Fresh formula must be mixed for each feed and all utensils must be clean to prevent contamination. You will need to have accurate scales and measures so that the quantities are correct. Formula must also be very well stirred so that the mixture is uniform and lump-free.

Cooking times should be in accordance with the instructions on the product. Food must be well mixed to prevent hotspots and cooled to the correct temperature before it is fed to the chicks. The required temperature is 100° Fahrenheit or 40° Celsius, which is just over human body temperature.

The degree to which formula is diluted is determined by the age of the chicks. Babies aged two to four days should only have a maximum of 10% solids in their food. This increases to 20 or 30% as the chicks get older.

Methods of feeding

Hand reared Parrotlet chicks are fed every few hours using a syringe; pipette; spoon; or a soft, rubber avian feeding tube. Metal feeding tools should never be used on very young birds as they can cause internal damage. Before any method can be employed, the chick must be persuaded to open their mouths and take food.

Fortunately, it's not too hard to elicit a feeding response in them. All you need to do is touch the chick's commissures, i.e. the area where the upper and lower beak join. The chick will open its mouth and begin bobbing its head. This motion closes the glottis so that food goes into the cop and not into the lungs.

Using a teaspoon:

The teaspoon can be a little easier to use if it is bent as this allows greater flexibility in terms of angle. The advantage of this method is that it requires increased handling which helps to tame the bird.

The disadvantages of this technique are two-fold. Firstly, this method of feeding formula to a chick is both time-consuming and messy. Secondly, dipping a spoon into the formula and touching the baby's mouth may contaminate the formula. If one chick is sick it may infect all the others in the clutch.

Plastic pipettes are an option for very young chicks. However, they only hold very small amounts of formula at a time, which means using them is time consuming. They also pose the same risk as spoons in terms of spreading illnesses.

Syringes have always been a popular and effective delivery mechanism for formula for baby birds. You need to use a catheter tipped syringe, tip the baby's head back when it's feeding response is present, and dribble the food into the wide-open mouth. You can also squirt the food directly into the chick's crop but only once you really know what you are doing. It is essential, though, not to squirt food into the mouth or crop unless the feeding response (head bobbing or pumping) is present or there is risk of getting food into the lungs.

The advantages of syringes are that you can easily control the speed of feeding and measure the quantity. Furthermore, they don't pose the same health and contamination risks because a syringe holds the correct amount of food and a new, clean syringe can be used for each chick. The syringes should be thoroughly cleaned and disinfected between feeds.

Feeding complications

If food is not the correct temperature or delivered to the chick at the right time or in the right way, medical complications can occur.

The first of these is a condition called crop stasis. In normal circumstances the crop will empty completely between feeds. If it doesn't, the food may sour or go off and become a breeding ground for fungi or bacteria. If the crop doesn't empty properly you need to take the baby to a vet to establish the underlying cause.

Hard lumps may also form in the crop if the water and solid matter in the formula separate. The treatment is to feed the baby a little warm water and *very* gently massage the crop until the lump dissolves.

The second hand rearing related health complication also affects the crop. It is called crop burn and, as the name suggests, happens when the formula is too hot. The baby's crop is burnt by the food and this can cause tissue death and / or fissures in the tissue. Overheating of formula seems to occur more often when microwaves are used. A good routine to follow is to allow the feed to stand for a minute, give it a thorough stir, and then use a thermometer to check the temperature.

The final feeding complication is aspiration. This is when food particles get into the buccal cavity or even the lungs of babies. The buccal cavity lies at the back of the mouth above the opening to both the oesophagus and trachea. This happens if chicks are force fed, over fed, have poor feeding responses, or there is pressure on a full crop if, for instance, the baby falls over and lands on the crop.

How much food to give a baby

Babies that are fed small amounts throughout the day and night will wean faster and, in most cases, be much healthier than those fed less often. They need a minimum an average of five feeds in a 24-hour period. A chick under three days old needs six feeds and older ones require four feeds. You will know the hatchling has had enough food when the crop looks rounded.

The crop should, as mentioned, empty fully between feeds. Babies have a small pouch of loose skin around the crop that allows the crop to stretch to accommodate food. Don't mistake this pouch as a full or partially full crop.

Once the crop is full it's advisable to place the chick into a small, stable container of some sort. This will prevent the baby falling onto the full crop and possibly aspirating as food is forced out of the crop.

Weaning

Regular feedings result in faster weaning. An outdated, unproductive, and unfeeling method of hand rearing is still used by some breeders. They only feed babies twice a day (morning and evening) in the belief that a hungry baby will move to solids / wean sooner. Because the babies are hungry they become stressed and are in fact less likely to wean quickly. They may also develop health and emotional problems.

It is advisable to introduce solid food such as vegetables and fruit into the nursery. Although the chicks won't eat them until they have been weaned, it is a good way to get the babies used to new foods. One can't go straight from formula to solids. There are a few options for very soft foods that can help to bridge the gap between formula and solid foods.

Some breeders have had success with coaxing chicks to eat soft foods in the form of steamed (and cooled) carrots, pumpkin, or sweet potato. Another option is commercial parrot food that has been moistened and softened with warm water. In either case, fresh batches must be made each day to prevent them spoiling and making the chicks unwell. In hot weather you may need to make a fresh batch twice a day.

As the youngsters eat increasing amounts of the weaning food you can decrease the quantity and frequency of formula feeds. The only exception is the night feed when a full formula meal should be given. You will know the youngster is almost weaned when it starts to refuse formula because its crop is full of weaning food.

Weaning is usually complete after eight or ten weeks although individual chicks wean at slightly different rates. The breeder needs to be patient and not force the process. If one does it could delay weaning or cause other complications.

There may be some weight loss during weaning. This is normal so long as it does not exceed 10 to 15% of the chick's bodyweight. If the chick loses too much body mass, it must be taken to a vet before it becomes ill.

Fledging

You will be able to see the blood moving up the shafts of the pin or flight feathers your young birds are growing. Once there is an inch or 1 ½ centimetres of blood still in the feather the young birds are ready to move into a cage where they can walk around, stretch their wings, and learn to use perches.

These youngsters are still uncoordinated so place the perches close to the bottom of the cage. If they do fall off or lose their balance they won't fall far and injure themselves. When all the blood in the feather has been absorbed you can place the fledglings into a larger cage that allows flight.

Sexing baby parrots

Parrotlet young are usually almost fully feathered by the time they are four weeks old. As a result, the sex markings on the rump and wings will be clearly visible which allows you to determine the sex of the fledglings. Sex markings may intensify in colour after their first moult.

Hygiene for babies

The main objective with cage hygiene is the prevention of disease. This is of course important with adult birds too, but chicks have underdeveloped immune systems and it takes time for normal, healthy gut flora to become established. This means that babies are particularly susceptible to infections of various kinds.

One needs to:

- ✓ Observe babies closely for signs of illness and / or stress
- ✓ Always keep their environment clean
- ✓ Avoid contamination or spoiling of food as discussed earlier
- ✓ Ensure that anyone handling the babies washes their hands very thoroughly beforehand and afterwards
- ✓ Handle very young chicks as little as possible.

Emergency care of day-old chicks

Chicks as young as a day old should be hand reared only in emergency situations. Because they can ingest so little at a time these babies must be fed every 30 or 45 minutes during the first 24-hours.

Breeders often dilute formula with an electrolyte solution instead of water until these high-risk infant birds are four or even five days old.

Record keeping

Keeping records of a feeding program for each clutch is a helpful and important activity. Each baby is weighed each morning and the result and date recorded along with notes about what the youngster is being fed. Growth rates are not the focus as much as health and progress in terms of the chick's physical development.

In addition to helping to identify babies that are not gaining weight and growing or losing too much body mass, these records help breeders identify which formulas and weaning foods are the most beneficial and successful.

The weighing also gives the breeder the opportunity to observe the baby for skin softness, plumpness, healthy pink skin, plump toes and rump, and symmetry (an asymmetrical body in babies is often a sign that they are malnourished).

Over time the feeding program and record keeping can be refined.

Chapter 12: Costs & where to buy a Parrotlet

The two most popular Parrotlet species – the Pacific / Celestial and the Green Rumped – are both available from breeders, pet stores, and speciality avian on-line shops. However, ensure that you are buying a bird from a reputable breeder or dealer. Both species are a good choice for a novice parrot owner.

The Spectacled and Yellow Faced Parrotlets are not as easy to come by. You may be able to order them or track down a pet bird through the Internet, regional or national associations, online bird or parrot clubs, or through an avian vet.

1) Costs

Depending on the species, you will pay in the region of $100 – $300 or £72 – £215 for a Parrotlet (and considerably more for a rarer colour). Be cautious when purchasing or rehoming a lower priced, "preloved" Parrotlet as it may be an older or unhealthy bird and you will have no way of knowing how well fed, healthy, socialised, and behaved it is.

Other once-off costs for a bird that will be a pet and not used for breeding include:

- A suitable flight cage: $69.00 - $414.00 or £50.00 – £300.00
- Food and water bowls: $5.50 – $16.50 or £4.00 – £12.00 each (it is recommended that you buy 2 of each)
- Toys: $2.75 or £2.00 each or £30 / $41.00 for a pack of multiple toys
- Cuttlefish: $4.80 or £3.50 for a pack of two
- Nesting box: $9.65 - $22.00 or £7.00 – £16.00
- Perches: $2.00 - $2.75 or £1.50 – £2.00 each.

Ongoing expenses such as food are hard to estimate because it depends on the diet you select for your feathered companion.

However, a bag of parrot pellets cost, at the time of writing, in the region of £7.00 or $9.65 for a 1 kilogram / 2.2 pound bag.

There are expenses that one can predict to a degree. But there are others such as vet bills in the event of illness or injury that can't be foreseen.

2) Tips on buying a Parrotlet

If possible, purchase a bird from a registered breeder. Ask an avian vet for recommendations about reputable breeders. Also, do some research on the Internet, as there are various associations and other official bodies that have this type of information. Joining Parrotlet groups, clubs and forums online is a wonderful and fun way to find information.

Avoid buying a Parrotlet that needs to be rehomed. You can often tell that this is the case because the purchase price will be very significantly lower than the usual market price. Rehomed Parrotlets are not a good idea, as most older birds won't bond with a new owner. As a result, they are far more likely to be skittish, shy or even aggressive.

Chapter 13: Conclusion

Parrotlets, regardless of species, can make wonderful companions and pets. However, as with any other pet they bring with them great responsibility that will last for many years.

1) Do's... in no particular order

✓ Learn about Parrotlets

✓ Make sure that your country, county, or state permits these little birds as there can be regional laws prohibiting certain pets in specified areas

✓ Take the time and the trouble to bond with your young Parrotlet and socialise it

✓ Get to know the way your pet behaves and looks as this will help you pick up quickly when it is not well

✓ Maintain socialisation by spending several hours with your pint-sized bird every day

✓ Start training early on, especially step-up, step-down, and recall training

✓ Establish a good relationship with the local avian vet

✓ Take your Parrotlet for an annual check-up

✓ Make sure you get a cage that is large enough for an adult Parrotlet and that allows for flight and play

✓ Ensure that your little bird can't escape from its cage or injure itself in it

✓ Change the toys regularly so that these bright, active birds don't get bored

✓ Feed your Parrotlet a good, varied diet

- ✓ Keep a First Aid Kit and contact list handy

- ✓ Ensure its cage is always kept

- ✓ Keep an eye on your Parrotlet so you don't accidentally stand on or injure it

2) Don'ts... in no particular order

- Don't adopt a wait-and-see approach if you suspect your feathered pet is not well. These pets can become critically ill very quickly

- Don't stroke your bird on the wings or down the back as this may trigger or encourage breeding behaviour

- Never give your bird a seed only diet or over-feed a baby

- Don't leave anything that is toxic or a choking hazard where a Parrotlet can get to it

- Shout at or punish your Parrotlet

- Ignore signs of ill health

- Leave your Parrotlet unsupervised when it is out of its cage.

3) And in closing...

This guide's primary purpose is to make sure that you have the information that you need to decide, first and foremost, if this is *really* the right pet for you, for your spouse, for your child or for your household.

If the answer is a confident and honest "Yes", this pet owner's guide will also give you the details that will help you to keep your Parrotlet healthy and happy.

All animals in captivity should at least live to their usual or expected life span. In fact, given they are safe from their natural predators and receive a good diet and vet care they should exceed the average life span for their species.

If you are one of those individuals who commits to owning, loving, and caring for one of these amazing little birds you will be rewarded by having a pet that is entertaining, intelligent, sweet-natured and beautiful.

Enjoy your Parrotlet and teach others about them!

Printed in Great Britain
by Amazon